A Shadow of the Past

Also by Mehru Jaffer

The Book of Nizamuddin Aulia
Book of Muhammad
Book of Muinuddin Chishti
Love and Life in Lucknow:
An Imaginary Biography of a City

A Shadow of the Past

A SHORT BIOGRAPHY OF LUCKNOW

MEHRU JAFFER

ALEPH

ALEPH

ALEPH BOOK COMPANY
An independent publishing firm
promoted by *Rupa Publications India*

First published in India in 2021
by Aleph Book Company
7/16 Ansari Road, Daryaganj
New Delhi 110 002

Copyright © Mehru Jaffer 2021

All rights reserved.

The author has asserted her moral rights.

The views and opinions expressed in this book are the author's own and the facts are as reported by her, which have been verified to the extent possible, and the publishers are not in any way liable for the same.

The publisher has used its best endeavours to ensure that URLs for external websites referred to in this book are correct and active at the time of going to press. However, the publisher has no responsibility for the websites and can make no guarantee that a site will remain live or that the content is or will remain appropriate.

No part of this publication may be reproduced, transmitted, or stored in a retrieval system, in any form or by any means, without permission in writing from Aleph Book Company.

ISBN: 978-93-90652-48-8

1 3 5 7 9 10 8 6 4 2

Printed at Parksons Graphics Pvt. Ltd, Mumbai

This book is sold subject to the condition that it shall not, by way of trade or otherwise, be lent, resold, hired out, or otherwise circulated without the publisher's prior consent in any form of binding or cover other than that in which it is published.

For Jaffar and Ali, who keep the flame of love, longing, and poetry alive in our conversations

Contents

Introduction / ix

ONE
A Garden of Eden / 1

TWO
Paradise of Poets / 38

THREE
Beyond Borders / 57

FOUR
The Honey-Tongued / 72

FIVE
Mad About Movies / 88

SIX
The World is My Oyster / 97

SEVEN
Making up Stories / 106

Acknowledgements / 123

Notes / 125

Introduction

I'm afraid there is nothing iconic about contemporary Lucknow. Except for crumbs left over from a very unique way of life which evolved about 200 years ago, there is little else to be found. Lucknow is better known now for its high pollution levels, low employment opportunities, and electricity and water shortages. The city has emerged in modern times as a tacky imitation of swanky metros elsewhere. Most of the contemporary architecture is unimaginative, public places are sub-standard, and the display of wealth by those who have it is garish. On Diwali, Lucknow is decked out in eye-hurting made-in-China lights. Most of the potters who made clay lamps by hand now earn their living as labourers at construction sites, or have been reduced to begging. Closed-door shopping malls built on rich agricultural land have rendered cultivators jobless. Builders have filled up the many water bodies with concrete to raise shabby marketplaces, discouraging migratory birds from returning to Lucknow.

Even memories of the spectacular life once lived here have blurred in the midst of a society with little regard for history or heritage. Some buildings from the past do exist but they are falling apart. No wonder people in Lucknow sigh a lot. Contemporary citizens cannot forget how grand Lucknow once was but it is getting more and more difficult to imagine that grandeur. That makes people wistful. It makes them sigh out of love and longing for the way the city was.

Lucknow was a glorious place to live in at a time when citizens treated each other well. Ordinary folks lived in close-knit communities and people stood by each other—in times of cheer as well as distress. Now life feels uncertain and there is a growing sense of alienation with familiar neighbourhoods slowly disappearing. The floating population that is in and out of the city is perhaps not as emotionally attached to either the place or the people like in the past.

That is why much of the narrative in this book is about the good old days. The attempt is to go as far back as possible, to the origins of a certain way of life that established Lucknow's reputation worldwide as a paradise on earth. In the late eighteenth century, Lucknow was transformed into an extraordinary habitat by people who were washed onto its shore by sheer circumstance. By the nineteenth century, Lucknow had become a world-class capital city because of a group of people. Without the vision and generosity of the people in power, a city is merely dust on the face of the earth. It is the people who pick up the dust and sculpt it into a habitat and breathe life into a city.

Asaf-ud-Daula is number one on the list of people responsible for making Lucknow unique. The fourth

a shadow of the past

ruler from the Nawabi dynasty of Awadh, Asaf-ud-Daula began his rule in 1775 and transformed this rustic trading port on the banks of the Gomti into a chic cosmopolitan city. His confidence in his rule and generosity encouraged talented people from different parts of the world to make a home in Lucknow. Indo-Islamic and European ideas merged here to make Lucknow a powerhouse of creativity. The court of the nineteenth-century rulers of Lucknow swarmed with European painters and photographers. In the third quarter of the eighteenth century, poets from Delhi's Mughal court migrated to Lucknow hoping for better remuneration. The rulers of Awadh were rich and powerful and lived at a time when the Indian subcontinent was making a shift from a traditional way of life towards modernity. Asaf-ud-Daula was a great patron of new ideas. His successors, too, allowed people to unleash their talent in Lucknow—for their own good and for the collective good of society.

In the nineteenth century, citizens appreciated each other and the peace and harmony that followed allowed commercial activities to boom uninterrupted. The practice of living and letting others live contributed to making Lucknow special. Much of that way of life has fallen by the wayside although the city continues to bask in a certain reputation that is fast fading. The truth is that time has watered down the quality of morality and ethics once practised in the city. The cuisine, fashion, sport, and language born out of mutual respect of one human being for another has also been affected for the worse.

This is a book about some of the people responsible for Lucknow's formidable fame. The hope is that it will inspire us to return to some practices that made Lucknow a city most liveable and lovable in the past. The book also features contemporary citizens. Despite all the angst that accompanies life in modern times, many citizens continue to struggle to make the capital city of Uttar Pradesh more people-friendly.

Most of the information in this book is from decades of reading everything available in print on Lucknow. Whichever corner of the world I have visited, I have searched archives and libraries of those places for information on Lucknow. In a bookshop in Bukhara, Uzbekistan, I found notes on Lucknow. I have consulted books catalogued at Austria's National Library in Vienna. In the end, though, the perspective about Lucknow is mine, and mine alone. Verses chosen for you from Urdu poetry are from books, but also from rekhta.org, the largest website in the world for Urdu poetry. The translations from Urdu into English are mostly mine, except where indicated. It is my dream to capture the elegance of Urdu poetry in English. Let me know, dear readers, if I have been able to do that for you or not.

ONE

A Garden of Eden

I often wonder at Lucknow's enduring reputation as some sort of Shangrila. In literature and in cinema, the image of Lucknow is that of an eternal Garden of Eden where nightingales sing without pause and innocence competes with buds to flower into ethereal memories.

How did Lucknow, one of India's most backward and chaotic cities today, earn such formidable fame? I think the culprit is the poet who has been painting an extraordinary picture of Lucknow since the nineteenth century.

Urdu poet Mir Taqi Mir, who died in Lucknow in 1810, describes the molten gold that drips down all doorways and walls of the city at every sunrise and sunset.

> shafaq se hain dar-o-diwar zard sham-o-sahar hua hai
>
> Lucknow iis rahguzar mein pilibhit

However, Lucknow's repute as a wondrous city without compare began to fade even before the nineteenth century ended. But wordsmiths have immortalized the goodness of Lucknow, making sure that consciousness of the past is ever-present, inspiring generations to continue to applaud their city.

Nazm Tabatabai, who died in 1933, waves an admonishing finger at the guard outside the Garden of Eden, warning him not to be proud of his abode but to know of praises showered upon Lucknow.

> gulshan-e-firdaus par kya naaz hai rizvan
>
> tujhe poochh uske dil se jo hai rutba-daan-e-lucknow

Today Lucknow is a pale shadow of its former glory but practices from the nineteenth century have deep roots. This has made it possible for contemporary citizens to occasionally glimpse bits and pieces left over from that golden age, whether it is in the kiss of the purvaiya, the gentle easterly breeze at sunset, in a morsel of biryani, or in the surprise repartee of a blue-blooded resident of Lucknow. Before the nineteenth century, Lucknow was little more than a bustling bazaar, just another trading post on the banks of the Gomti. Trade boats ferrying goods between the coastal areas of the Bay of Bengal and the agriculturally rich heartland of the Indian subcontinent had made this place a hub of enviable commercial activity. Lucknow was always rich in trade. However, the place was rustic in appearance. Most of the land around Lucknow was split into small fiefdoms owned by many, often warring, landlords. After he chose

a shadow of the past

Lucknow as his capital in 1775, Asaf-ud-Daula, the city's first monarch, infused aesthetics into the hectic agricultural activities of the grain market, transforming it into a sophisticated seat of government. Soon, Lucknow's eminence as the home of an increasingly urbane population spread far and wide.

Asaf-ud-Daula had inherited a lone fort on one of the many hillocks along the banks of the river. Known as Macchi Bhawan, Asaf-ud-Daula's great-grandfather had captured the fort in 1722 from the sheikhzadas, a family of local landlords.

The common ancestor of the sheikhzadas was Sheikh Abdur Rahim, who built the fort in the sixteenth century, having received Lucknow and the lush fields surrounding it as a gift from the Mughal emperor Akbar. Below the fort was a crowded market and the area was congested with the houses of wealthy merchants and poor peasants. Neither Asaf-ud-Daula nor his descendants lived in the fort. It was used as an armoury. During the 1857 War of Independence, the fort was blown up by the British, destroying all the ammunition and firearms stored there. For nearly half a century, the hillock lay covered in thick Lakhnawi dust. In the early twentieth century, local landlords raised funds to clear the debris and to build the King George Medical University and Hospital on the ruins of Macchi Bhawan. Today, the hill is bustling with thousands of medical students and even more patients from all over the country. The imposing façade of the medical university from 1911 is designed in the Indo-Saracenic style and painted a glistening white, as if forever washed in moonlight. The campus has been immortalized on screen by director Mira Nair as Brahmpur University from Vikram Seth's novel, *A Suitable Boy*. Nair spent the entire autumn of 2019 in Lucknow, filming the award-winning novel for the BBC.

Asaf-ud-Daula was the fourth in a line of eleven rulers over eight decades. The patriarch of the Nawabi dynasty was an economic migrant who found employment in Delhi as a soldier in the eighteenth century. He was born in Nishapur, Khorasan, in modern-day Iran and was given charge of the Mughal emperor's territory in a region which had Faizabad as its capital. This was two decades before the birth of Asaf-ud-Daula in 1748.

Asaf-ud-Daula's love for poetry was a gift from his ancestors. He married his passion for classical Persian poetry with folk music and the language spoken by those living in and around Lucknow. Asaf-ud-Daula was born in Faizabad. He never travelled to Iran but learnt to appreciate Persian poets like Nizami and Saadi. The Persians were so passionate about poetry that even scientific treatises were often penned in verse in medieval times. Dr Mostafa Vaziri, Iranian physician and anthropologist, told me that the eleventh century polymath Ibn Sina wrote a metrical treatise on medicine. Nasir Khusraw, from the same century, poetized the human anatomy in his writing. Asaf-ud-Daula studied the Khorasani style of lyricism of Manuchehri, the eleventh century court poet from Persia. The verses of Persian poet Hafiz Shirazi put him in touch with his emotions, and he loved the mysticism in the verses of Sufi poets like Fariduddin Attar.

At the age of twenty-six, Asaf-ud-Daula was a reluctant heir. He seemed unprepared to take on the responsibilities of a ruler. He would have preferred to travel and study poetry. Since the responsibility of governance was forced on him, Asaf-ud-Daula decided to govern poetically. He imagined Lucknow not merely as another dot on earth but as a poem. Asaf-ud-Daula peopled his city with those belonging to different breeds and creeds, making it a tiny mirror image of life itself that thrives on diversity. He wanted his court to be more gorgeous than any other. He gave the architects around him free rein to transcend the grandeur of the buildings in Delhi, and to make each creation memorable. While his father had lived in a temporary tent city in Faizabad, Asaf-ud-Daula built Daulat Khana, a permanent residence for himself in Lucknow. Most parts of the Daulat Khana have now crumbled but the Bada Imambara, Asafi Mosque, royal water tank and bath, and the Rumi Gate remain the pride of the city and are great tourist attractions.

A confidante of Asaf-ud-Daula was Claude Martin, a French officer whose grand mansion is one of the best preserved buildings from the nineteenth century. In 1840, this mansion was converted into a school—La Martinière College. It ranks as one of the top schools in the country today. Art collector and engineer Colonel Antoine-Louis Henri de Polier was a friend of Shuja-ud-Daula, father of Asaf-ud-Daula. Polier also worked for Asaf-ud-Daula. He was fluent in Hindustani and Farsi and his interest in Indo-Persian culture led him to put together numerous manuscripts and works of art. Polier was friends with British painters William Hodges and Johann Zoffany. He discovered local artists in the many by-lanes of Chowk Bazaar, the congested marketplace of the late eighteenth century. He dived into the hustle of the narrow lanes of the main Chowk Bazaar, in step to the sound of silver being beaten into thin wraps for sweetmeats. Behind embroidered shirts and waistcoats, hookahs and shoes, and perfume and silver jewellery, he found artists sitting and painting in the midst of spices and the aroma of fresh jasmine.

Polier chose local artists from the Chowk Bazaar and taught them European painting techniques at workshops organized by him.

Polier returned to France in 1788 after more than three decades in India, leaving behind his fascination for archiving information with the people of Lucknow. When he moved back to Europe, the collection in his private library was divided between libraries in Paris, London, Berlin, and Lausanne. Much of what we know about Lucknow is from information archived by Polier at that time. This love for libraries is still alive in Lucknow. One of the oldest libraries was built in 1882 and still stands. The Amiruddaula Library

a shadow of the past

has a collection of 200,000 books in Sanskrit, Hindi, English, Urdu, Arabic, Persian, and Bengali. The Tagore Library is part of the Lucknow University campus. It was designed by Walter Burley Griffin, the American architect of the Australian capital, Canberra. Griffin saw splendour in Lucknow when he lived there for about fifteen months before his sudden death in 1937. He designed an art deco building for *The Pioneer* that was pulled down in the 1990s without any thought for heritage, and his grave in a Lucknow cemetery is difficult to find, buried as it is beneath overgrown grass.

The formal education introduced at various workshops from the late eighteenth century in Lucknow culminated much later in the founding of the Lucknow College of Arts and Crafts in 1911. The doors of the Bhartendu Natya Akademi opened in the 1970s to satiate the city's love of theatre. Today, the list of the alumni of Lucknow's theatre academy is long, and many of these stars illuminate the silver screen—Nawazuddin Siddiqui, Anupam Kher, Rajiv Jain, Rajpal Yadav, and Nalneesh Neel are just some of them.

Dance, drama, and hyperbole are still an integral part of daily life in Lucknow, including the narration of charming stories such as this one:

Some two centuries ago, a favourite garment made of fine muslin cotton from Dhaka suffered a tear. The owner of that garment was inconsolable. A darner was found who promised to undo the damage. A few days later, the garment was returned in one piece. The tear had been embroidered over with a lovely motif in white thread on the white muslin cloth that was lighter in weight than the feathers of a dove. That is believed to be the beginning of the white-on-white chikankari work which Lucknow is so famous for. In Farsi, the word 'chikan' means embroidery, and this art had once earned much appreciation and wealth for the local artisans. From around 1860, the arrival of industries distracted people from agricultural activities and handicrafts. Ever since then, the fate of farmers and artisans has been uncertain.

Design academician and social entrepreneur Jaspal Kalra is trying to recapture for artisans the respect they once enjoyed in Lucknow. He works to empower artisans through education. Kalra is from Lucknow and has a PhD in 'Design Education of Chikankari Artisans: A Tool for Social Innovation' from Mohali's National Institute of Fashion Technology (NIFT). After a post graduate degree in design from Nottingham Trent University, he returned to Lucknow as director of the Kalhath Institute founded by the Lucknow Design Trust in 2017.

There was a flood of Bengali migration to Lucknow at the turn of the last century. After the British annexed Lucknow in 1856, educated and professional Bengalis found jobs in the railways, post, and telegraph offices, and as teachers and physicians. Bengali localities sprouted all over the city.

One of the most illustrious Bengali migrants to come

a shadow of the past

to Lucknow at the turn of the last century was Atul Prasad Sen. He built a flourishing law practice in the city and was a well-known composer of Bengali songs called atulprasadi. Sen deeply influenced the cultural life of the city. After his death in 1934, a road was named after him on which a host of Bengalis built colonial style bungalows. The Kalhath Institute is housed in one such bungalow that was built by a Bengali family who sold it decades later to a local politician.

The institute opened in a former residence as a place for the formal education of artisans. In the bargain, a heritage building has been saved in a city that shows remarkable disregard for its cultural legacy.

Talk to Jaspal Kalra and he will remind you of a tradition in Lucknow that is thousands of years old and of those times when handicrafts were considered to be economic and cultural assets. Crafts were a luxury in the past. In recent times, the price-conscious mass market is incapable of appreciating handicrafts even in a place that is the cradle of exquisite handmade goods like chikankari, kamdani, and zardozi. Other crafts that Lucknow was famous for but which are dying include weaving, printing, pottery, glassware, woodwork, and masonry. During extensive field research, Jaspal Kalra found that artisans are marginalized, lack proper wages, have poor negotiating powers and recognition, and that their socio-economic status is low. The Kalhath Institute works with whatever is left of the local craft communities, both men and women, to enhance their confidence in craft practices, and gave them financial independence, and social well-being.

In another attempt to revive crafts in the city, fashion designer Asma Hussain rescued the first floor of a building in the historic Hazratganj area from collapse. In the year 2019 she was honoured by the Lucknow chapter of the Indian National Trust for Art and Cultural Heritage (INTACH). Asma Hussain renovated the dilapidated premises in 1994 to house the city's first Institute of Fashion Technology which became home to a spectacular collection of rare garments embroidered in chikankari, zardozi, muqaish, and tukdi. Her forte is the fusion of the traditional art of sewing with modern motifs, even on western-style clothes. Her maternal grandmother is a direct descendant of Bahu Begum, mother of Asaf-ud-Daula.

'My grandmother was a great storyteller. She taught me a lot about fashion through numerous stories about the family,' says Asma Hussain, whose most prized possession is a hundred-year-old wedding dress belonging to an elderly relative. While the institute imparts both practical and theoretical training on fashion, the fashion house is a retail and design outlet, and a manufacturing unit for traditional embroidery that is used to embellish tailored garments. There is also a corner reserved for students to showcase their creativity and skills honed at the institute.

A democratic environment allows many more individual entrepreneurs to display their expertise

a shadow of the past

now. Lucknow has a long history of recognizing the talent of people belonging to different continents and cultures. Indo-Islamic and European ideas merged to make Lucknow a powerhouse of creativity throughout the nineteenth century. The court of the later rulers of Lucknow swarmed with European painters and photographers as well. In the third quarter of the eighteenth century, poets from Delhi's Mughal court migrated to Lucknow in the hope of better income. Mir Taqi Mir left Delhi for Lucknow in 1782 and he died there in 1810.

Lucknow's architectural heritage includes places of everyday use like public gardens and parks. On public demand, a stone bridge came up across the Gomti in the late eighteenth century. Some thirty years earlier, in 1843, an iron bridge had been built using the parts that an engineer had brought from England.

From the early nineteenth century, successive rulers of Lucknow expanded the city eastwards from Asaf-ud-Daula's residence, the Daulat Khana. The court moved from the Macchi Bhawan to the Daulat Khana, then to the Farhat Baksh, or pleasure-giving palace, built in the Indo-French style in 1781. A few years later, the Chattar Manzil, or palace of umbrellas, was built. Today, the Farhat Baksh and Chattar Manzil stand side by side on the banks of the Gomti, slowly being reduced to ruins.

Although born at the Chattar Manzil in 1822, Wajid Ali Shah, the last ruler of Lucknow, chose to live in Qaiserbagh, the palace complex he began to build in 1840. He was twenty-seven years old when he succeeded to the throne and conceived Qaiserbagh as a paradise on earth. It was a sprawling residential area with beautiful gardens, marble pavilions, and fountains perfumed with fresh rose petals.

The Qaiserbagh palace complex was completed in 1850 and became a temple of those cults of wit, gaiety, and licentiousness that made Lucknow a city most envied throughout the country.

Once a year, the gates of Qaiserbagh were opened to the public when Wajid Ali Shah allowed ordinary citizens to experience night-long performances of dance and music. His favourite was a dance drama about Krishna's youth in the verdant surroundings of Vrindavan in the company of love-lorn gopis. The role of the gopis was played by professional dancers who lived within the Qaiserbagh palace complex and Wajid Ali Shah played Krishna.

An oblong enclosure within Qaiserbagh included a row of elegant and imposing two-storeyed homes. One of the wings of the complex was pulled down by the British when they reorganized Lucknow into a colonial city after winning the First War of Independence in 1857. After vanquishing the locals, the British gifted the other three wings of the royal residence to local landlords who supported them. Some buildings from that time still stand but are in shameful neglect, while the Qaiserbagh area is reduced to just another noisy, traffic-infested neighbourhood of Lucknow.

a shadow of the past

By the nineteenth century, the rulers of Lucknow were no longer warriors or farmers. Their status was reduced to majestic men of leisure, practising an exaggerated art of politeness and living off revenue collected from the hinterland by experienced members of a well-oiled bureaucracy. The rulers had mortgaged their independence and had paid the British through the nose for protection. In the 1770s, they lost vast areas of territory to the British, like the Fort of Chunar, and later Benaras, Ghazipur, and the Allahabad Fort. The defeat in the Battle of Buxar in 1764 had shattered the confidence of the army. Shuja-ud-Daula was even forced to sign a treaty with the British in 1768 that limited the size of his army and, by 1785, the royal army had degenerated into a useless institution. However, there was no dearth of money that kept flowing in from the countryside, inviting more migrants to make a living in Lucknow. At the dawn of the nineteenth century, Lucknow was famous for the study of science, theatre, literature, and the arts. The sun had set on medieval times and Lucknow welcomed modernity with open arms.

The Firangi Mahal, the house of foreigners, was built near the Chowk Bazaar in the seventeenth century. In 1647, it was a home for European visitors who had permission from the Mughal ruler in Delhi to visit Lucknow for the purpose of trade. During the reign of Aurangzeb, the palatial building was confiscated and gifted to the Shaheed brothers, who were scholar-friends of the emperor. Mullah Asad bin Qutab Shaheed and his brother Mullah Saeed bin Qutabuddin Shaheed converted a large part of the house into a seminary that gradually began enjoying a reputation equal to Cambridge and Oxford universities in England.

Between the seventeenth and twentieth centuries, the seminary developed the Nizamiya syllabus with a focus on rational science studies. Lessons in logic, Persian, Greek philosophy, mathematics, and the art of calligraphy were taught, keeping in mind the social, cultural, and technological changes taking place at that time. People from all over the world came to study here and many an alumnus of Firangi Mahal was appointed to important posts in the city's judiciary and bureaucracy. Although the Firangi Mahal has lost its grandeur, a visit to the premises is an awe-inspiring experience. The place is falling apart but people continue to live there and Adnan Abdul Wali Firangi Mahali is always glad to greet visitors. Adnan is the great-grandson of Maulana Abdul Bari Firangi Mahali. Mahatma Gandhi and the Maulana had worked closely for Hindu–Muslim unity. A well-known story has it that Gandhiji brought his goat to stay with him at the Firangi Mahal. Out of respect, the residents gave up meat as long as Gandhiji was their guest. Adnan has letters from Gandhiji to the Maulana, as well as the wooden footwear that the Father of the Nation used while at Firangi Mahal.

Adnan has little to say of the recent achievements of the Firangi Mahal, but he is full of stories from the past. He points to the room used by Gandhiji in the early twentieth century. He is happy to show people whatever is left of the home built by his ancestors even though it reflects a state of poverty and neglect today.

As a wealthy centre of commerce and manufacturing, Lucknow attracted traders, warriors, and spiritual leaders to its shores. Muslim mystics followed Hindu fakirs into the heartland of India where the Bhakti movement of local poets and wandering yogis was already a force. The oldest shrine of a mystic in Lucknow is that of Shah Mina, who was loved by ordinary people because he was kind and compassionate beyond words. His abode at the base of where Lucknow's prestigious medical university now stands was called Mina Nagri in the fifteenth century.

This good man was born in 1397 in Lucknow, and was called Muhammad Mina by his elders who followed the spiritual ways of the Chistiya and Suhrawardi schools of mysticism. Later, his devotees named him Shah Mina and he was beloved for never allowing anyone who visited his humble home to go without a meal. Shah means 'king', and mina is 'fish' in Sanskrit, 'light' in Arabic, and 'love' in Pashto. Shah Mina is all of the above and much more to his devotees who visit his shrine in large crowds to this day.

It is not unusual for pilgrims to pray at the shrine of Shah Mina and then walk down to Kudia Ghat on the banks of the Gomti. This part of the river is sacred from the time before Shah Mina, because Rishi Kaundilya, a holy man, is believed to have meditated here.

The nineteenth century saw the skyline of the city redrawn with the silhouettes of newly-built mosques. When the British came to power after 1857, many churches, too, dotted the skyline of the city. The number of men breeding elephants and horses multiplied in Lakshmanpur, one of the prehistoric names for the wholesale market on the banks of the Gomti that, by the nineteenth century, had evolved into a multicultural metropolis called Lucknow. Agricultural wealth helped to landscape the city into a lush garden, and to bloom into a centre of high culture. Travellers came here from different corners of the globe out of curiosity to confirm whether stories of the luxurious lifestyle they had heard about were true or not. According to Premchand:

> All Lucknow was steeped in the pursuit of luxury...while some favoured soirees with music and dancing girls, others dedicated themselves to intoxication, to opium. But in every department of existence, entertainment and pleasure reigned supreme. Whether in the administration, or in the field of literature, in the arts as in commerce, in everyday living itself, indulgence had become the norm. Employees of the state dedicated themselves to the pleasures of the flesh, poets sang of love and of the pangs of separation, craftsmen turned out fine embroidered fabrics, tradesmen provided cosmetic refinements, perfumes and rare unguents.

a shadow of the past

Different people brought different things to Lucknow—animal skin, animal fur, gunpowder, the latest technology, religions, and new ideas of the origin of the world. In return, they took spices, grains, gems, ivory, sugar, and perfumes. Of all the goods that travelled to and fro, the journey of the Urdu language is the most poetic. A large group of courtesans and poets came to Lucknow to earn their living. They brought Urdu with them. The seed of colloquial Urdu was sown in northern India. But the language travelled to different parts of the country like Hyderabad and Gujarat. On the way, it enriched itself with a wide range of vocabulary picked up from the local languages and those spoken by Turkic, Persian, and Arabic people before it evolved into a classical language in the court of Delhi. By the time it returned to Lucknow in the nineteenth century, the imperial court was ready to replace Farsi with home-grown Urdu. In the leisurely ambience of a decaying Lucknow, Urdu found ample opportunity to perfect its role as the sweetest medium for expressing powerful emotions.

Don't miss the wicked warmth in the verses of Asrarul Haq Majaz Lakhnawi who introduces himself to the world as an enigma. He continues:

Love is all, and his only need.

Love, and only love is his desire but the mind introduces logic that begins to tire.

Majaz was born in 1911. He was six years old when the 1917 revolution in Russia was successful and affected global politics in a big way. The abdication of the monarch in Russia was celebrated worldwide as the end of the centralized rule of the monarchy. People sang and danced on the streets not only in Moscow but also in Paris and London at the prospect of a more democratic life in the future. Majaz grew up, convinced that real power rested with ordinary people, and not with a single ruler. He was born into a feudal family of landlords in Rudauli, in the countryside, a two-hour drive from Lucknow. Ideas of love and equality of all human beings were dear to him and a gift to his conscience from his Sufi ancestors. A modern education at the Aligarh Muslim University (AMU) made it easy for Majaz to merge humane Oriental values with global ideas of equality, liberty, and fraternity, making him one of the most progressive poets of all time. He was intolerant of a society that was dominated by a small, privileged elite basking in splendour. The idea that the poor of the country could force the exploiter out of their lives had lit up his imagination.

Majaz was the ultimate romantic. The poet saw Lucknow as a utopia, a place of beauty and love and the lap of grace. Majaz wrote that more poems bloom in the city than flowers. Lucknow was home to many a race. Maidens here, he felt, were the envy of Cleopatra. Every corner filled with crowds. Poets proliferated in very corner of the city.

Asaf-ud-Daula encouraged citizens to appreciate poetry and elevated Lucknow to a city of learning. He had spent a great deal of his time with writers and poets and poured out his own grief in verse. He says that in the lanes of idols all that he, Asaf, can see night and day is the carnival of Khuda, Creator of the world.

buton ki gali meiin shab o roz Asaf
tamasha-i-khuda ko hum dekhte haiin

The people of Lucknow loved Asaf-ud-Daula's poetry but they loved him more as a generous ruler.

'Jisko na de maula usko de Asaf-ud-Daula' is a saying still popular in Lucknow, meaning when God forgets to propose, Asaf-ud-Daula is there to dispose.

Asaf-ud-Daula died in 1797. At the time he passed, shops in the main bazaar of Chowk over flowed with goods and piles of gold and silver. Every lane in the local market was filled with fragrance from the perfume of crushed rose petals and jasmine flowers. The heady aroma mingled with savouries fried in clarified butter. Colourful pottery, embroidered cloth and shoes, metalware in which precious stones were embedded in exquisite patterns attracted buyers. Those workshops have vanished. The lanes are now empty of flower shops and perfumeries have been reduced to tiny stalls here and dusty stands there. Most of the shops are tucked between drains overflowing with filth, constantly released from homes in the overcrowded neighbourhood. There is no rice sold on Chawalwali

Gali inside the Gol Darwaza, and all the eateries have disappeared from Bawarchiwali Gali. Most of the former cooks now run catering businesses instead. At the Bawarchiwali Gali, it is difficult to find a kebab, but plenty of business cards are handed out to those passing by in case they need caterers for the next party hosted in Lucknow. Fine muslin cloth, cotton cloth, gold, and silver have been replaced by nylon and zinc in the ground-floor shops that still line the bazaar in Chowk. The living quarters above the shops have changed beyond recognition. In the past, the balconies the of first-floor apartments, where the courtesans lived, were hidden away from the inside rooms by finely ribbed bamboo curtains. Hindi novelist Amritlal Nagar lived all his life in a rented eighteenth-century home in Chowk. He called himself the self-styled vice chancellor of Chowk university, as he documented everyday life in the neighbourhood in his numerous novels. He talked to real-life courtesans and immortalized their stories in *Yeh Kothewaliyan* in 1960. The book is a precious treatise on the dreams and aspirations of women who continued to live above the shops in the crowded marketplace of Chowk, trying to make a living in the midst of society that refused to recognize their existence. Nagar writes that the nineteenth-century tawaif or courtesan was not a prostitute. She did not sell just sex, but made life worth living for the elite, by sharing with them her talent for poetry recitation, classical music, and delightful conversation. And she was respected in the

a shadow of the past

nineteenth century for her contribution to society.

Dr Deeksha Nagar, a fifty-two-year-old ethnographer and folklorist and granddaughter of the novelist, told me that her grandfather could not have written *Yeh Kothewaliyan* without the support of his wife.

'As a child, I recall being told by Baa (Grandmother) about the vocational school for the women of Chowk's red-light area on the terrace of her home. The women had lost their livelihood in contemporary times and no one wanted to employ them. Baa got them to learn sewing and embroidery and taught their children to read and write. There is a precious photo, in a family album, of Baa surrounded by a group of children, probably being taught by her. Seen in the photo sitting with the children from homes in the red-light area is my father's youngest sister,' says Deeksha.

Baa introduced the women from the infamous red-light area of Chowk to the children in the large joint family of the Nagar household simply as aunts. The women saw Baa as an elder sister, and called her Baaji. Baa would offer them tea and betel leaves as they talked to Amritlal Nagar about the problems they faced. It was only years later, when Deeksha was a teenager, that she realized that these women, whom she had called aunts, were the mothers, daughters, and granddaughters of the courtesans who had inspired her grandfather to write *Yeh Kothewaliyan*.

Deeksha also remembers Kallu, Muniya, and Munni, children of sweepers who cleaned the non-flush toilets in the Nagar home in Chowk. This family of sweepers was interviewed by Amritlal Nagar as well and appears in another novel titled *Nachhyo Bahut Gopal*. How can she ever forget Kallu, Muniya, and Munni, who were always there to help her cross the narrow lane of Mirza Mandi whenever an aggressive cow or a bull stood in the way? These are sweet memories that Deeksha carries with her as she shuttles between India and the USA, where she now lives with her husband and son.

Writers like Amritlal Nagar and Majaz inherited their love for humanity probably from values passed down to them from the previous generation. 'Be humane and love fellow human beings dearly' is the spirit found in every line written by them, inspiring those around them to do the same.

In *Chaudhvin ka Chand*, a 1960 film, lyricist Shakeel Badayuni pens a breathless tribute to Lucknow comparing it to a beautiful garden. Badayuni writes that another name for Lucknow is paradise.

> So lively, lovely and vibrant is the earth, home of youth and verse, land of letters.
>
> The city in bloom, love in every heart, the season of spring never far apart. Where florets flirt, traditions mirror taste, every branch home to a nightingale in song, streets alive with steps of glee and the spirit never wrong.

Badayuni was born in a place located a little west of Lucknow. He graduated from the Aligarh Muslim

University and wrote verses for Hindi cinema, set to music composed mostly by the Lucknow-born music director, Naushad. Badayuni was a musician at heart and Naushad's love for Urdu poetry combined to give glorious music to Hindi cinema. Naushad came from a conservative Muslim family that did not approve of dance and music. In a feudal society, members of elite families did not entertain. It was their privilege to be entertained by professional entertainers. There was an entire community of entertainers called bhaands who were hired by the elite to perform for them. As Western-style style education modernized minds and feudal forces weakened, people from 'respectable' families, too, took up acting, singing, and dancing as careers.

The age of theatre and cinema had dawned, and the Royal Theatre in Aminabad was now a cinema house. It was situated close to where Naushad lived in Lucknow. In the 1930s, the theatre began to screen silent films. Naushad was very passionate about music, and he made the theatre his second home. As a teenager, he earned one rupee per performance for playing the harmonium between shows of films. The arrival of the talkies got Naushad even more excited, and before he turned twenty, he ran away to Mumbai in 1937. For a long time, his family in Lucknow did not know what Naushad did in Mumbai. When he returned to the city for his wedding, the band belted out popular songs from *Rattan,* the 1944 blockbuster. However, none of his elders realized film. Much of the music and first-class poetry in the early years of Hindi cinema owed their origins to Lucknow.

Lucknow-born English/Urdu poet Salman Akhtar is Majaz's nephew. In 1953, Salman's thirty-seven-year-old mother, Safia, Majaz's older sister, passed away. After his mother's death, the seven-year-old Salman continued to live in Lucknow in Darul Seraj, a sprawling bungalow built by Chowdhry Seraj-ul-Haq, his maternal grandfather. For a few years, Salman went to school in Lucknow. In 1973, he left for further studies to the USA, the memories of his ailing mother weighing more than the luggage allowed on transatlantic flights. As a child, he had watched helplessly as disease devoured his mother. He grew up to study medicine so that he could help others combat ailments. Salman is a practising psychiatrist today. His poetry is mainly about nostalgia and a longing to live in India by a river. The river imagery is close to his heart because he grew up in Lucknow beside the Gomti. Javed Akhtar, Salman's older brother, is one of the most loved lyricists of the land. During one of his visits to Lucknow, Javed told me that the secret behind the success of his songs is Urdu and the fact that he was brought up in Lucknow.

Salman visits Lucknow whenever he can, mostly in search of a feeling that he is familiar with from his childhood. He looks forward to sampling the city's delights and especially looks forward to meeting other poets. In a verse, Salman hopes that during a visit to Lucknow, he will be able to forge a hundred more

a shadow of the past

relationships. Poetry is important to him as it dissolves pain and lights up the dark crevices of his heart.

The less poetically inclined might wonder what Salman Akhtar is talking about. To them, Lucknow is a provincial town, boring, chaotic, and overcrowded. For at least the first two decades of my life, I, too, saw nothing except the heat and dust in Lucknow. After acquiring a fine primary education at La Martinière Girls College and a postgraduate degree from Lucknow University in the 1970s, I could not wait to flee Lucknow. It was, perhaps, not enough to cruise around the city on a bright red sports bicycle, and prepare for a future in the Indian administrative services. As far as I was concerned, Lucknow did not have enough buzz to stimulate me. Life was boring in Lucknow, where the streets built by the British were still broad, clean, and quiet. There were plenty of pavements and it was not unusual to walk to school in Shahnajaf from my home in Lawrence Terrace.

At the time of Independence in 1947, the population of Lucknow was about 4 lakh. Today, it is nearly 4 million. Lucknow is the capital of Uttar Pradesh, home of cut-throat politics and murderous real-estate activities. According to the National Crime Records Bureau (NCRB) report released in 2020, Lucknow had the maximum number of cases of crimes against women amongst nineteen cities, with 2,736 cases being reported in 2018.

It is the new normal for readers to wake up in

Lucknow to headlines like 'Bullets Fly in Hazratganj, Whizz Past Woman'. Hazratganj is a century-old market which the British spruced up in imitation of London's Oxford Street. It is a place where people go to meet each other. The tradition is for people to dress up in their best and stroll up and down the one-kilometre-long avenue, often only to meet friends. The ritual is called ganjing, and those who perform it experience inner joy at the thought that in the midst of friends all can only be well. But, not all is well in Lucknow today. That is why the country's most populous state is often called 'ulta pradesh' or the upside-down province where the population has increased to millions of people without employment opportunities keeping pace. Other essentials like infrastructure, healthcare, and literacy are wanting. Citizens had once exchanged pleasantries in love letters ferried by snow-white pigeons. Now, messages shared on WhatsApp often make citizens suspicious of each other. There is no room in the city for entertaining the woes of ordinary citizens. There is no room for talk of revolution and rebellion against social injustices either. The main concern of the rich and powerful is to segregate and polarize people.

Siddharth Varadarajan is a Delhi-based journalist who grew up in Lucknow in a South Indian family on values based on the Indian Constitution. Today, he talks tirelessly against those who want to divide citizens on the basis of religion. He finds this kind of politics ugly and dangerous. It is painful to watch some citizens bullied, mocked, and provoked by others in a city that is traditionally shy of participating in conversations that promote hate. The present-day attitude is disgraceful and against the ethos of the city. After all, unity amongst its citizens is the backbone of Lucknow's Ganga-Jamni tehzeeb, the art of coming together like the confluence of two rivers. Trying to turn one citizen against another is not tehzeeb, civilized behaviour, and shows no tameez, discretion, and is definitely not a sign of development. Can the spread of hate ever be an option for a city built on mutual respect and coexistence?

When Lucknow is called a city of culture and refined living, the reference, perhaps, is to the exalted times that existed between the end of the eighteenth century and the middle of the nineteenth century. Lucknow's lifestyle has never again been as illustrious as it was during those years, until the British annexed the city in 1856. The courteous way of life and prosperity recorded till then has not returned. Instead, life in present-day Lucknow is shabby in comparison. It was only 200 years ago that the region was still flush with funds from landholdings and trade, and the constant ebb and flow of human beings from different civilizations had given birth to a very unique Indo-Islamic culture. The nineteenth-century rulers of this land found strength in unity amongst the people they ruled. They came here as warriors but gave up war to sow seeds of love in the soil.

Wajid Ali Shah, the last ruler of Lucknow, who died

in 1887, is the author of around a hundred books. He was a great poet and artiste. His autobiography, written in 1849, is titled *Ishqnama*, the Chronicle of Love. As I have said, he designed and built Qaiserbagh, a palace complex and architectural fantasy, as his home. The king conceived Qaiserbagh as an earthly version of a garden in paradise. It was a complex of palaces, courtyards, gardens, pavilions, tombs, and royal bazaars that were later knocked down by the British out of envy and for revenge. According to Ranjit Hoskote, author and cultural theorist, had Wajid Ali Shah been European, he would have been acclaimed as a nineteenth-century artistic visionary. Every year, he would open the gates of Qaiserbagh to the public and invite citizens to participate in a pageant led by him. Irrespective of caste and religion, everyone in the city was invited to dress in saffron robes like a yogi. These events hosted regularly by the ruler helped to dissolve the differences between the ruler and the ruled, and the fear of citizens for one another.

For Rosie Llewellyn-Jones, author of *The Last King in India: Wajid Ali Shah*, the numerous events regularly held by royalty were important landmarks in getting the diverse population of the city to better appreciate each other. Lucknow gave access to learning not just to the elite; liberal ideas were shared with all the citizens. Everyone was encouraged to think philosophically, to take time in composing conversations poetically, and to live in love and peace with each other.

a shadow of the past

Manzilat Fatima is from the family of the Shia Muslim rulers of Lucknow. Her father is the grandson of Birjis Qadr, son of Wajid Ali Shah and Begum Hazrat Mahal, who led the War of Independence against the British in Lucknow in 1857. The war broke out a year after the British dethroned Wajid Ali Shah, who left for Kolkata with a large enough entourage to create a mini-Lucknow on the banks of the Hooghly, in a neighbourhood called Matiaburj, the hillock of mud. He lived here for the next three decades till his death in 1887. In Kolkata, Wajid Ali Shah was first provided accommodation at the British East India Company's Fort Williams where he complained of too many mosquitos. So he was housed in the quiet suburb of Matiaburj, about four miles away from Kolkata. Once Wajid Ali Shah moved to Matiaburj, his court with its many wives, menagerie, and servants woke up the sleepy suburb and turned it into a lively but close-knit community of people who lived there as if they had never left Lucknow.

Birjis Qadr was poisoned in 1893 at Matiaburj. Since then, this branch of the royal family has not lived in the neighbourhood. A law graduate, Manzilat studied at the Aligarh Muslim University, where her father was a reader. Now, in her fifties, she lives on Mirza Ghalib Street in Kolkata. A few years ago, a friend who visited Manzilat sighed with satisfaction after eating a meal at Manzilat's home. She pointed out that what was regular food for Manzilat was special and not easily available. This is heritage food, the friend had said to Manzilat. That got her thinking. She gave up law to open Manzilat's, an eatery in Kolkata where she serves delicious Awadhi food from recipes that have been passed down in the family. Knowing how popular Manzilat's, her terrace restaurant, is, when Manzilat came to my place in Lucknow for dinner, I made sure to cook the basmati rice biryani with mutton and garnish it with saffron threads. It was an evening most pleasant, except when Manzilat fell silent at not finding any potatoes in the biryani.

Herein lies the difference between Kolkata biryani and Lakhnawi biryani. After Wajid Ali Shah settled down in Matiaburj, his kitchen experimented with roasting whole potatoes and adding them to the traditional Lakhnawi biryani. Today, the mutton biryani in Kolkata is unimaginable without potatoes. Meanwhile, Lucknow takes pride in refusing to corrupt the royal biryani by adding the humble potato to it.

∽

A flood of followers of Islam, mostly from Central Asia, together with the local population, helped to landscape Lucknow in a colourful mix of designs and styles—Islamic and European. The buildings were not very tall and were separated by narrow, crooked streets that were crowded with people, and led to one colourful market after another.

a shadow of the past

Edward Hilton, who defended the Residency during the first War of Independence, died in Lucknow in 1922 and is buried in the ruined premises of the Residency. He wrote two guide books on Lucknow. In a *Tourists' Guide to Lucknow*, written in 1899, he wrote:

> The bazaars were abundantly stocked, the population was literally teeming, so that it was impossible to ride, or drive in the streets, save at a walk; the people generally were cleanly dressed, betokening that they were living under a regime, which placed the common necessaries of life reasonably within the reach of all classes; but the melancholy and memorable events of 1857 and 1858 have reduced the number of handsome houses by one half, whilst the trade and manufactures, for which, in all their riches and variety, Lucknow was once so famous, have all but disappeared. Nevertheless, to compensate for this apparent deterioration, there are now many fine broad streets, many excellent marketplaces, improved ventilation, good drainage and seemingly a more equable and healthy air of prosperity may well be hoped for, especially when the traffic becomes developed by the completion of the Avadh and Rohilkund network of railways. The traveller may then bid farewell to the crumbling mosque, the deserted garden, the ruined fountain, the remains of palaces, seraglios

and all the marks of the reigns of the kings of Avadh. Lucknow will gradually assume its former prosperity as the veritable capital.

That is why the British coveted Lucknow. Once Lucknow was annexed by the British, all the agricultural wealth and riches earned in markets became a jewel in the crown of the ruler of England. The local people were frustrated at being colonized. Local storytellers recited an exaggerated version of Lucknow's pre-colonial history in public places. The nostalgic trend to amplify the goodness of the city before the British spoiled it all began in colonial times to give solace to citizens who resented the rule of the colonialists. The storyteller of every dastan took it upon himself to create such twists and turns in his narration that would help calm the nerves of a city under siege. This was the raconteur's way of healing society by talking of an idealized past as an alternative to an unpleasant present. The oral tradition manipulated the imagination of the listeners to create a magical world.

Tilism-e-Hoshruba is the world's first fantasy epic written originally in Urdu by Muhammad Husain Jah in the late nineteenth century. It has been translated into English by Musharraf Farooqi. This text was very popular with professional storytellers in Lucknow, who continued to convince audiences that their city was still the most enchanting place in the world. The art of the storyteller whose words had transported people into a world of illusion was destroyed by the rise of rationalism, technological inventions, and alternative forms of entertainment, like the radio, in the early twentieth century. It has seen a revival now and is popular in Lucknow and elsewhere.

Says a dastango:

> The beauty of Princess Bahar was so astonishing that even charming fairies were fit only to be her slave girls. Her hair was a net for the birds of lovers' souls; it entrapped the hearts of her admirers helplessly in its locks.

It's not the history books but storytellers who inform us that people have lived in Lucknow since the Vedic times and that the place had prospered under the Gupta dynasty between the fourth and sixth centuries. It was always an attractive destination for migrants from different corners of the globe. One of North India's greatest rulers, King Harsha, made Kannauj his capital in the seventh century, but he realized the importance of Lucknow as an important gunj—a treasure house of grains. Later, quarrels over land between the three powerful Hindu kingdoms of the Rashtrakutas, Pratiharas, and the Palas converted the green fields of the Indo-Gangetic plain into a bloody battleground. Eventually, wars reduced the area to wilderness and it remained forgotten for a couple of centuries.

In the twelfth century, Bijli Pasi, a fiercely independent local peasant leader, cleared large swathes of the jungle for cultivation. To consolidate his power, Bijli called himself maharaja, and built twelve forts in and around Lucknow. He ruled from the nearby city of Bijnor. Although belonging to one of the lower castes, Maharaja Bijli Pasi is the founder of the Pasi dynasty of rulers and tales of his valour are part of the folklore of this place. One of the many legends about the origins of Lucknow goes back to another Pasi. Many Dalits believe that Maharaja Lakhan Pasi founded the city called Lakhanpur, which, over time, became corrupted to Lucknow. However, others say that Lucknow is named after Lakshman, brother of Rama, the legendary ruler of Ayodhya. Awadh is the Persianized pronunciation of Ayodhya. After Lord Rama sent his wife, Sita, into exile, she was escorted from Ayodhya by Lakshman to Bithoor, where Valmiki, sage and author of the Sanskrit Ramayana, had his hut. On the way, Sita and Lakshman rested on a hillock beside the Gomti in Lucknow. This is still known as Lakshman Tila. It is in Bithoor that Sita gave birth to the twins, Luv and Kush.

Daldeo was the last great ruler of the Pasi dynasty of peasant princes—he was overthrown by Rajput warriors and, later, by the armies of the rulers of the Delhi Sultanate. The Pasis have been engaged in agricultural activities since antiquity. To this day, they claim to love and to know much more about the earth than others. In recent times, this traditional community of peasants has been relegated to the lowest rank in the society and counted amongst the Scheduled Castes. They are found mainly in the agriculture-rich states of Bihar and Uttar Pradesh.

For his hostility against the British, Maharaja Bijli Pasi was demonized under the Criminal Tribes Act of the British government. The ultimate punishment for this son of the soil was to prohibit him from owning land, to declare him a natural criminal, and to destroy all records of him and his family members as rulers of the land. However, it is not easy to hide what is obvious. The ruins of a fortification built by Maharaja Bijli more than a thousand years ago are witness to the majestic past of the Pasi rulers. One fort was built in Lucknow on the road to Bijnor. Little more than a few broken pillars and parts of its ancient walls remain on a slope that is largely abandoned. An early morning visit to the uneven landscape in the heart of Lucknow's overcrowded and noisy Ashiana neighbourhood is a sight to behold. While human beings continue to doze, and the dark of the night is undecided about breaking into light, dozens of peacocks descend upon a fiefdom that once belonged to the Pasi rulers. At that hour, a chorus of birds is heard, as if desperate to share what they know about life. The place provides an idyllic moment to ponder over the irony of existence. The present-day plight of the Pasis is an amazing example of the eternal see-saw of life where a pauper may end up as a prince and a baron forced to beggary.

For a moment in contemporary times, it had seemed

that Mayawati, head of the Bahujan Samaj Party, was destined to return power to the majority population of Scheduled Castes. Three-time chief minister of Uttar Pradesh, Mayawati has built imposing memorials, parks, and statues in red sandstone and in the name of Dalit icons, including herself. Today, large structures dominate the skyline in the southeast part of the city across the river from Chowk. The imposing buildings of Mayawati are a symbol of Dalit pride and have helped Lucknow regain some of its visual grandeur as a capital city. From my home in Gomti Nagar, where housing complexes have mushroomed mostly in imitation of American-style condominiums, I took a ride in an Uber to Hazratganj recently. On the way, I talked to Raj Kiran, the twenty-seven-year-old driver. He belongs to Behta, a village a few kilometres from Lucknow. He comes from a family of traditional peasants and has inherited 18,000 square feet of agricultural land which he tills between 5 a. m. and 8 a. m. Around 9 he hits the road as a taxi driver. He drives for about twelve hours every day before returning to his village at night. He grows wheat and rice, potatoes and peas, and seasonal vegetables. He sells his produce at the open-air grain market held every Tuesday and Saturday in Behta.

'If the price of wheat in Lucknow is ₹25 per kilo, at the Behta markets it is ₹18. People come here from neighbouring villages to buy grains and other rations, like pulses,' says Raj Kiran. There are stalls selling vegetables, toys, utensils, shoes, and clothes, but this traditional market, one of the oldest and biggest, is most popular for the sale of grains. Raj Kiran recalls his elders telling him that, a long time ago, the villagers would harvest their crop and sell it in wholesale markets in Lucknow. But, ever since local markets, like the one in Behta opened, farmers save money and time by selling goods at their doorstep. Few open-air and wholesale markets remain in Lucknow today.

The rulers of Lucknow were lords of an independent kingdom in the nineteenth century and no longer in service of the Mughals. It was the dream of the British to end Mughal rule in Delhi and to govern India directly. By the early eighteenth century, Emperor Aurangzeb was dead. He was the last Mughal emperor to exercise real power. After Aurangzeb, decadence and weakness ruled Delhi.

Historian John Pemble wrote in *The Raj, The Indian Mutiny and the Kingdom of Oudh 1801-1859,* 'Effeminacy, cupidity and treachery tainted the Muslim aristocracy of Delhi; provincial governors asserted their independence; and religious factiousness divided the Muslim community. The empire thus fell a swift victim to the dangers that were besetting it from within and without.'

The fall of Delhi only made it easy for Lucknow to replace the Mughal capital as the new hub of learning, power, and wealth.

TWO

Paradise of Poets

As usual, the three friends had little better to do than to loiter around lanes that were lined with trees taller than the skyscrapers. At this time, Lucknow was still famous for the baghs, those lush gardens laid out all over the city. Every day, the friends had followed the same routine. After sunset, they would step out of their home in Lalbagh to aimlessly walk towards Charbagh. Often, they would stop in the middle of the road to figure out how they had reached Alambagh instead. They were forever lost in heated conversations that made them forget their way. Once, they had to turn back from Telibagh and it took them hours to return to Qaiserbagh because they had passed by Badshahbagh instead of Sunderbagh. Their favourite stroll remained around the leafy surroundings of Sikandarbagh.

On a particular day, the same thought had troubled all of them. They wondered why so many dogs in the city were called Tipu in the Lucknow of the late 1930s.

The boys were in their early twenties and railed against British rule in India. Majaz was the eldest, and he was the angriest of the three vagabonds. He paused on pavements to kick stones so hard that his feet bled. He would stand under a streetlight, shaking his head over the slavish mentality of his fellow Indians. When Indians named their dogs Tipu, did they even know what they were doing? They just did so in imitation of the British. Many English families in Lucknow had called their dogs by this name to mock and demean Tipu Sultan, the eighteenth-century ruler of the kingdom of Mysore and bitter enemy of the British. Ali Sardar Jafri, the second of the threesome, wanted to do something to revenge this injustice to the memory of Tipu Saheb, the great freedom fighter. Syed Sibte Hasan, the youngest of the three, listened to his friends express concern and disappeared for a while. When he returned several hours later, he held an adorable snow-white puppy in his arms that he introduced as Nelson. The puppy got his name from Horatio Nelson, the most admired British admiral in the eighteenth century.

Jafri mentions this incident in a slim book titled *Five Nights of Lucknow*. Jafri returned to the city in 1937 after he was expelled from Aligarh Muslim University for his anti-British views, and for keeping company with communists. Those were heady days in Lucknow. The scent of freedom from colonial rule was in the air, and Jafri's decision to live here proved fortuitous. The atmosphere of the city was such that it taught him to dream of a bright future for Indians, especially the poor. Lucknow made a poet out of the twenty-year-old Jafri who matured into one of the most progressive Urdu poets of all time. Born around 200 kilometres away in Balrampur, in the countryside, his stay in Lucknow had fanned Jafri's patriotism. Today, Jafri is loved for having used his mind to pen poems from the heart like this one:

> Revolution will come, don't let its pace distress,
> it is not slow what seems not to hurry.

Lucknow became a hotbed of political activity and home to numerous social activists and professional politicians. Freedom fighters and politicians made a lot of noise in Lucknow and refused to be silenced.

Awadhi, a local dialect, was spoken here. After the arrival of Farsi-speaking Turkic and Mongol warriors, the vocabularies of the local people and the classical Farsi language together gave birth to Urdu. Throughout the decades of struggle against the British, many a wall in the city was smeared with Urdu graffiti saying: 'Hai Akhtari!' (a sigh for beloved Akhtari) and 'Inquilab Zindabad' (long live the revolution).

In the twentieth century, Urdu vocabulary did not focus on the self-centred concerns of the elite. The language was free from the confines of the four walls of the court and had cascaded down into the hearts of ordinary citizens. Urdu had made romantics and poets of many on the streets. Then, it was not unusual to come face-to-face with a poet walking down a footpath, lost behind shelves in a popular bookshop, or holding forth at a roadside tea stall. Moin Ahsan Jazbi spent

a shadow of the past

a considerable amount of time with Ali Sardar Jafri in Lucknow. Poets like Jafri and Jazbi belonged to the Progressive Writers' Movement and had freed their writing from classical clichés, thereby giving ideological content to the poetry they wrote. The new love of these progressive writers, who were also fighting for freedom from the British, was their country. In defiance of British rule, Jazbi had publicly recited:

> crush the world of sorrow and heart's agony
> this is a new love, a new obsession,
> and God knows what I should do with it.

Jafri's constant companion was Majaz, the people's poet who adored Lucknow and praised his hometown in Urdu verse:

> Paradise of love and beauty,
> lap of grace,
> is Lucknow.

The city's youth at the time were intoxicated with hope for a less oppressive and more egalitarian future—they drank to that future in the taverns that dotted the city.

Sang Majaz:

> This joyful assembly so rapturous,
> this gathering so luminous,
> revellers left holding glass in hand,
> I downed it all, spilling some.

Syed Sibte Hassan, before migrating to Pakistan, in 1948, worked for *The Pioneer* in Lucknow, and for the *National Herald* in Allahabad. In his book, *From Moses to Marx*, he confessed that he had 'learnt the first principles of socialism from the prominent revolutionary historian, the late Kunwar Mohammad Ashraf. Those were the days when the British were in power in the country and there was no visibility of socialist literature anywhere in India.'

Ashraf was a Marxist historian, and political secretary to Maulana Abul Kalam Azad and Jawaharlal Nehru, senior Congress party leaders and freedom fighters. The Moradabad-born Ashraf left his studies at the Aligarh Muslim University to join the more radicalized campus of Delhi's Jamia Millia Islamia. Jamia was founded as a national university, in 1920, by Dr Zakir Husain, the third president of India, and shifted a few years later, from Aligarh to Delhi. The campus was cosmopolitan and had Hindu and Christian teachers. Some of the staff came from Germany where Husain had studied at the University of Berlin in the roaring 1920s. Then, Albert Einstein had lived in Berlin as part of a large, expanding community of scientists during the tumultuous interwar era. This German capital was a citadel of left-wing politics and coveted by fascist forces. Socialist leader Dr Ram Manohar Lohia was a student in Berlin till 1933. He was in Berlin when the fascists finally overpowered the communists. After a fever-pitch campaign, the fascist party was victorious in the German

a shadow of the past

national elections and breezed into parliament in 1930. Voters during the interwar days were desperate for roti, kapda, aur makaan in a Germany weighed down by a terrible economic depression. It was easy to woo voters with woolly promises of employment, prosperity, and the revival of Germany's glorious past. In 1933, Lohia watched Adolf Hitler become the chancellor. When Indian students like Zakir Husain and Ram Manohar Lohia returned home, they brought with them news—both good and bad—from Europe. Notes were exchanged with fellow Indians and the thick fragrance of anti-fascist and progressive ideas wafted out of the Jamia campus to overwhelm the entire country. In Jamia, Sibte Hassan and Hayatullah Ansari chaired the Study Circle; secret meetings were held in the home of Professor Bashiruddin. Later, the Study Circle was shifted to Lucknow where the university campus was filled with political activists. Ashraf was part of the Study Circle and shared socialist and communist literature, banned by the British, with everyone. An appalling state of poverty all around them had aggravated resentment towards the British and attracted concerned citizens to socialist ideas.

Majaz addressed the students in verse:

> Don't wait for the revolution, be revolution,
> be fury, fire, lightning, and cloud,
> to make even death with your radiance proud.

During the troubled years of World War II, the doyens of Urdu literature found comfort in the company of each other. Ale Ahmad Suroor, Akhtar Hoshiyarpuri, Hayatullah Ansari, Khwaja Ahmad Abbas, Ismat Chughtai, Saadat Hasan Manto, Jazbi, Sibte, Jafri, and Majaz were all convinced that it was possible to overthrow British imperialism using socialist and communist ideas. This hope was shared amongst freedom fighters in prose and poetry. Suroor found poetry sharper than a sword. Poetry, he said, does not lead to revolution but creates a perfect environment to bring about sudden changes.

Once again, it was Majaz who spoke out the loudest:

> Speak up, oh earth, speak
> that the imperial crown begins to creak.

By the mid-1930s, Lucknow was a sanctuary for an increasing number of politically active youngsters. Many of them were poets who sang songs of social justice, and inspired society to wake up to the social and political realities of the day. All talk about resistance and struggle, exploitation and oppression, justice and equality, and exploitative systems sounded attractive in the Urdu language. Religion was the last thing on the minds of these youngsters. They defined religion as a private meditation between individuals and their beliefs. The progressives were convinced that religion no longer united people and did not provide social stability in society.

a shadow of the past

Josh Malihabadi was born in 1898 in Malihabad, near Lucknow. He wrote:

> My purpose is change, my name is youth,
> revolution, revolution, revolution is my cry and
> my truth.

Hayatullah Ansari's *Hindustan,* a national newspaper, was a powerful voice in support of the anti-colonial struggle. Ashraf wrote many books that influenced students and readers in search of alternative ideals to the decaying feudal order of which Lucknow was such a stronghold. Centuries of kingship and colonial diktats had propelled Lucknow to the status of a grand imperial city whose pomp and show had made it the envy of the world. However, the state of the majority of the population remained wretched. By the early twentieth century, many a dreamer of dreams concluded that enough was enough. They were convinced that Lucknow could become a refuge for all the tired and poor of the country. The dream was to do away with Lucknow's regal reputation, and turn it into a home for all the huddled masses yearning to breathe. Those were the days when it was a matter of pride to be a socialist in Lucknow. It became a passion with all thinking people to understand and practise progressive, secular, and socialist politics. 'Liberal' was not a bad word.

In Lucknow, Jafri, Majaz, and Sibte Hassan lived under one roof in a modest rented house. They called their home October House. This was in honour of the people's revolution in Russia in the same month, in 1917, led by the revolutionary leader Vladimir Lenin. They had a cook called Muhammad, who had little choice but to sometimes fast and sometimes feast along with his youthful employers. Muhammad had the unenviable task of running the kitchen on the erratic earnings of the trio. At one time, the writers earned money by editing and publishing *Parcham* (flag of revolution). The weekly tabloid was popular for its patriotic poetry and features, inspiring readers to remind the greedy that all human beings are entitled to the riches received from the generous earth. Later, the same boys edited a weekly, *Naya Adab* (new way of life). *Naya Adab* was read widely by intellectual giants of the time like Dr Rashid Jahan, Sajjad Zaheer, Ismat Chughtai, Munshi Premchand, and Saadat Hasan Manto, all budding authors and progressive thinkers.

One day, *Naya Adab* sold really well. That was the day when Jafri, Majaz, and Sibte Hassan returned home after many hours at work, hungry and exhausted. At the doorstep they were welcomed by appetizing aromas drifting out of their sparsely-stocked kitchen. The sound of kebabs sizzling on the frying pan was music to their ears.

'How come?' they asked Muhammad. The cook told them that a postman, had deposited a money order for ₹300 that day. The money came from a mass subscription for *Naya Adab* by factory workers in Kanpur. After the postman left, Muhammad had gone on a shopping spree. When the boys returned, he pulled out a drawer on a side table, and with great glee showed them where the rest of the money was kept.

When Muhammad was no more, a female sweeper instructed the boys in cooking from the kitchen window. The sweeper was not allowed into the kitchen as she belonged to the untouchable caste. She entertained the boys with her talk and her colourful vocabulary made them laugh. Her loving care thoroughly spoilt Nelson who was regularly bathed and groomed by the sweeper.

Numerous visitors of repute were constantly in and out of Lucknow in those days. Some of the inspirational ones included Mohandas Karamchand Gandhi and Jawaharlal Nehru. The Progressive Writers Association (PWA) held its first conference in 1936 at the majestic Rifa-e-Aam Club, built in the 1860s for the happiness (rifa) of ordinary Indians (aam) who were forbidden entry to the clubs run by the British. The Rifa-e-Aam Club, now reduced to a garbage dump, was the venue of many significant political and literary meets. It hosted the joint session of the Congress and Muslim League in 1916, when the historic Lucknow Pact was signed for a united front against the British.

Founded by communist leaders Faiz Ahmed Faiz, Sajjad Zaheer, and novelist Mulk Raj Anand, the PWA brought politicians, poets, dramatists, and filmmakers under one roof. In his address to the inaugural gathering of the PWA Munshi Premchand had overawed the audience with his views on the purpose of literature.

He said that a writer observes life. It is the job of a writer to examine life critically and truthfully. Without that, writing does not matter, nor does it endure. At this meeting, a message was read out from Rabindranath Tagore that stated that literature that is not in harmony with mankind is destined for failure.

The concerns of the PWA were not only literary but also included everyday problems faced by ordinary people, whether economic, cultural, or social. At that time, the appeal of the PWA was magnetic. It was a movement second only to Gandhi's countrywide call to participate in satyagraha, inspiring the masses to make demands for their rights without ever relinquishing the truth.

Much later in life, after Jafri had moved to Mumbai, he had this to say about the early days of the PWA:

> This Progressive Movement was a spectrum of different shades of political and literary opinions with Premchand, a confirmed believer in Gandhism at one end, and Sajjad Zaheer, a confirmed Marxist at the other end. In between them were various other shades including non-conformists, but every one of them interested in the freedom of the country and glory of literature.

In Lucknow, Jafri mostly met with people who shared a common commitment with the man on the street. This group of people was in love with the idea of freedom for all human beings, and in one voice had opposed

a shadow of the past

the exploitative values of feudal society.

In 'The Song of the Hands', Jafri sings in praise of the everyday miracles created by artisans, craftsmen, and labourers:

> Touched by these hands, clay turns to gold...
> respect these hands,
> venerate these hands,
> they make the world go round, these hands
> salute these hands.

The socialists had no time for the shenanigans of feudal lords and local monarchs, and had zero affection for British rule. A large number of people had joined the ballooning freedom struggle against the British. Lucknow had played host to the Indian National Congress that had met in the city, in 1936. The forty-six-year-old Nehru's address at the meet—a passionate plea for land reforms and for equal rights for all workers, including peasants, men, and women—had fired the imagination of the youth and idealists.

Jafri wrote in Urdu:

> Blood calls
> Everywhere is the call
> At dawn, at dusk, in silence, or in noise
> In a procession of mourners or at a meeting of revellers
> Blood calls

Jafri's ability to recognize social problems sharpened

during this time. He dreamt of a more just society after Independence. In a poem called 'Awadh ki Khakh-e-haseen', the poet is unable to contain his love for the earth that gave birth to him:

> My home, each particle of dust of my home,
> will receive even that drop of blood left, after
> the bloodbath.

It was not surprising that a mountain of historic injustices was being addressed in Lucknow. After all, the seed of many an economic, social, and cultural problem was sown here and numerous battles fought over territory by a line-up of kings, feudal lords, and, later, by the English. It was only expected that solutions be harvested in the same place where numerous problems had spread like weeds in the region.

In the early twentieth century, every aspect of life—from tradition to religion—was under the scanner. At this hour in history, progressive politics had imagined a world where social justice would reign supreme and where all human beings would enjoy equal rights and opportunities. The socialist idea of the world had no place for privilege-grabbing religious heads, kings, queens, landlords, and imperialists. And the collective sigh of the majority of people suffering centuries of exploitation, oppression, and injustice had become a roar that seemed impossible to ignore. It was feared that the fertile farmlands around Lucknow would once again be bloodied as the war waged against foreign rule became ferocious. Freedom fighters could not wait for the British to leave so that the poor could witness a new dawn of opportunities.

Inspired by political events and social movements around the globe, Lucknow addressed its historical injustices with courage. Here, discontent over feudal practices was unwavering. Combined with the inspiring politics of Gandhi, the socialist values of the Russian Revolution were a huge inspiration to all those who wanted a more just society. Those against communalism, caste practices, and landlordism that did not allow peasants to own the fields they tilled, followed Gandhi.

Most Gandhians wore homespun khadi clothes and Gandhi caps. In 1937, Jafri did the same. To express his youthful cockiness, he tilted the Gandhi cap on his head a little more to the left.

Jafri, Majaz, and Sibte Hassan carried Nelson with them wherever they went, and especially barged into places where the British had forbidden Indians and dogs to enter.

Mayfair was a cultural hub in the heart of Hazratganj. It had opened in 1939 with a restaurant, tea-house, and a cinema hall on the ground floor. The dress circle was an elevation with rows of seats arranged in a semi-circle, at the opposite end of the screen, giving the cinema hall an opera house kind of feel. On the first floor there was a ballroom with a live band for the entertainment of British residents in Lucknow.

One day, the three friends collected enough money to buy tickets for a film show at Mayfair. Nelson was now a big, handsome dog. Naturally, they were stopped at the entrance and told that dogs were not allowed into the cinema hall. The boys wanted to know the reason behind it. After all, they had a ticket for Nelson too! Nelson responded by adding to the commotion and barking non-stop. The manager was called and he talked to the boys in vocabulary dipped in sugar. He invited them for tea and returned the ticket money. The boys stepped out of Mayfair with Nelson and stopped to greet friends on the pavement. Just then, a soldier appeared in full uniform and began to tease Nelson with his baton. Nelson barked at the soldier. The boys tried to stop the dog from barking by shouting in one voice, 'Nelson, Nelson, Nelson'. Hearing a dog being addressed as Nelson, the inebriated tommy came after the boys. A crowd collected and began punching and kicking the British soldier. The punching and kicking dragged on from Mayfair towards the General Post Office building, at the other end of Hazratganj. For thirty minutes, the mob marched to the force of flying fists and to the tune of curse words and cries of 'Nelson, Nelson, Nelson...'

Eventually, the tommy surrendered and was allowed to waddle away from the crowd, with the promise that he would return the next day to the same place for a real wrestling match.

Majaz found the retreat of the soldier most

inspiring, and in a loud voice, he recited from his still incomplete composition:

> Speak up, oh earth speak
> that the imperial crown begins to creak.

Majaz placed Nelson on a chair and, picking up the soldier's dusty cap from the ground, parked it on Nelson's head, still singing…

This was the spirit of Lucknow in the early twentieth century. The people had not forgotten the humiliation suffered in the 1857 war against the British. Promises of relief from tyranny and oppression in Europe had fanned the imagination of all those dreaming of a more compassionate world. Many had received their first lesson in revolt against colonialism in schools and universities run by the English. The victory of the Russian peasantry in the 1917 Russian Revolution had filled the hearts of freedom fighters here with hope. The mood of vagabond poets like Majaz and Jafri was upbeat as they composed verses in defence of the downtrodden. The yearning for a more just world in Lucknow, the imperial capital, and a stronghold of feudal activities for centuries, was so powerful that it even penetrated the veil of anonymous women hidden behind male-dominated, orthodox Muslim families such as those living in the Firangi Mahal. Pick up any literature on Firangi Mahal and the reader is rewarded with a long list of male scholars from as far back as the seventeenth century. There is plenty of information available in print about the life and wisdom of men, without any mention of the female population of Firangi Mahal. It is only recently that the world has come to know of Sughra Fatima who hosted female-only literary events in the 1940s in Firangi Mahal. While male poets like Majaz and his fight against depression are well documented, it was nearly forgotten that Sughra Fatima composed and published poetry around the same time in Lucknow. At the age of thirty-nine, Sughra succumbed to mental illness and not many would have known about her if it wasn't for *Ek Inquilab Aur Aaya: Lucknow 1920-1949*, a documentary film screened recently in Lucknow. The film remembers Sughra Fatima as a glowing example of a woman who dissented and resisted both the politics of the day and patriarchy within the confines of a strict orthodox structure. Unknown to the rest of the world, the high literary life led by women inside Firangi Mahal in the early twentieth century has been recreated in the film. This is a tribute to Sughra Fatima who provided a platform in her home for women to express their intellectual and personal concerns despite the oppressive conditions of their existence.

Film director and feminist historian Uma Chakravarti stumbled upon the story of Sughra Fatima by accident. She wanted to film women who were jailed for their political activism before 1947. During this search she found Khadija Ansari, a sociologist jailed as a teenager by the British for her participation in the freedom movement. Khadija is Sughra Fatima's niece and was brought up in Firangi Mahal where women were born, married, and even buried within the same space without ever knowing what the world beyond their walls looked like. But Khadija refused to lead this life. She did not veil herself and rode a bicycle to school. She joined the Communist Party and participated in public agitations against the British on the streets of Lucknow in the 1940s. At the age of sixteen, she walked out of Firangi Mahal to marry a fellow communist who was a Hindu. She taught sociology at Delhi University's Miranda House. An octogenarian now, she lives in Bangalore. When Uma visited the Firangi Mahal with Khadija, she heard so many inspiring stories about Sughra Fatima that she decided to make a documentary on her and her niece.

However, Firangi Mahal was not always so conservative. It was built during the reign of Emperor Akbar as the home of a Frenchman who traded in horses. The palatial building also served as a guest house for traders from the East India Company who flocked to Lucknow to buy indigo, sugar, and cotton-cloth for sale in England. Because the building had hosted Europeans, the local people called the neighbourhood the palace of foreigners, or Firangi Mahal. Once trade slowed down, the Europeans did not return to the mansion in Lucknow. Emperor Aurangzeb confiscated the building and gifted it to two brothers who belonged to a Muslim family of clerics. In 1695, the clerics converted a part of the palace into a centre for Islamic learning. For the next two centuries, the reputation of Firangi Mahal soared as a liberal syllabus called the Dars-e-Nizami introduced intensive studies in logic, philosophy, mathematics, and Islamic jurisprudence. The open, inclusive reputation of the cosmopolitan campus travelled beyond Lucknow and attracted scholars from different parts of the Muslim world, including the Middle East, Turkey, and southern Spain.

After the annexation of Lucknow by the British, Firangi Mahal fell into neglect. Interest in the Arabic and Persian languages declined as English became the preferred language of the elite. However, Firangi Mahal played an active role during the freedom struggle as it hosted Mahatma Gandhi while he was in Lucknow. Leading clerics at Firangi Mahal were threatened with the death sentence for declaring a jihad or decree of revolt against the British government. In the early twentieth century, Firangi Mahal swarmed with nationalists, and many practising Muslims were also attracted to progressive, Communist ideas of social justice, equality, and freedom for all human beings.

The revolutionary energy of the time was infectious. It had cast a spell over the city and had percolated into the bloodstream of all those who lived here.

THREE

Beyond Borders

Just like the world descends upon Lucknow, people from the city have also wandered away to far-off lands, each one for a different reason. Imagine the joy of bumping into Dr Ghaus Mohiuddin Ansari in Austria's capital, Vienna! Dr Ansari was a Firangi Mahali. He graduated in Anthropology from Lucknow University after having received his primary education in Islamic Studies in Chowk, the oldest part of Lucknow. He was a descendant of Mulla Nizamuddin, the third son of Mulla Qutubuddin, one of the brothers who received the Firangi Mahal as a gift from Mughal emperor Aurangzeb. It is these brothers who converted the Firangi Mahal into a centre of learning, combining Islamic studies with modern-day science.

Mulla Nizamuddin designed Dars-e-Nizami, theteaching curriculum for the seminary at Firangi Mahal that became a model for Islamic studies all over the Muslim world. The syllabus was designed for higher education in Arabic and Persian but was unique for including lessons in law, logic, and mathematics as well. Dr Ansari was proud of his family. During long conversations in the cold and dark winter nights of Vienna, he also expressed regret at the intellectual stagnation that had gradually clouded life and learning at Firangi Mahal around the time of his birth in 1929. He left for London in the 1950s, and in 1957 had earned a PhD from the University of Vienna on caste practices amongst the Muslims of Uttar Pradesh. In that post-war period, interest in the social sciences was at its peak. The freedom to think and to engage in research-based education was the demand of academia along with the political freedom to vote and discuss issues of public interest. Lessons in the social sciences had become important. All democratic politicians and progressive regimes around the world were attracted to the social sciences and looked to the subject to help them formulate public-friendly, state policies.

It was even considered glamorous to study Social and Cultural Anthropology. Dr Ansari was coaxed by mentors to look at the society in his part of the world in a scientific way and to examine the complex relationship amongst the citizens within that society. The University of Vienna opened in 1365 with a focus on religious studies, but in the 1950s, it was a campus overflowing with socialist ideas. As the influence of medieval ideas of the church and the Pope declined, the campus was expanded and, over a period of time, transformed into a crucible of fresh thoughts. In 1945, the socialists had wrested the badly-bombed campus from the fascist and anti-Semitic regime of the defeated Nazi Party. A scholar of Jewish studies was responsible for resuming classes on campus in the summer of 1945 at the end of World War II. The free education policy in the post-war period of the socialist government had created an admission boom and students had come from all over the globe to study in Vienna. Dr Ghaus Ansari was one of them.

I met Dr Ansari in the 1990s. He had retired as Professor of Urban Anthropology and lived on Ottakringer Street in one of Vienna's many mass-housing complexes built by the Socialist Party of Austria. He spent the winter months in Vienna and, in the summer, he enjoyed life at his villa in the ancient fishing village of Calpe on the Mediterranean coast in southern Spain. He sometimes visited Lucknow. Off and on, he curated semesters on some aspect of Islam at the University of Vienna.

In the winter of 1991, I attended Dr Ansari's classes on Islam in South Asia at the university's ethnology department. Being a journalist with a postgraduate degree in English literature, this was my first formal lesson in history. Sitting in the heart of Europe, I was delighted to note fascinating details about the Mughal dynasty and about Delhi. By the time Dr Ansari's classes ended, I had fallen in love with history. Meanwhile, Dr Ansari had become a friend. When the semester was over, I was often invited to his Vienna home where I also met Dr Wadia Taha Najim, his Iraqi wife, who was a and professor of Arab literature. The three of us talked over gallons of tea. The street where the Ansaris lived cut into the Balkan Mile neighbourhood, named after its one-mile-long area thickly populated by people from the Balkans, including a large number of Turks. Dr Ansari chose to live here due to the lively multicultural feel of the neighbourhood, reminding him of the life he had left behind in Lucknow. The simmering tension combined with everyday bonhomie amongst the largely Muslim population of Turks and the Christian Slavs kept him connected to the spirit of the multicultural Indo-Islamic way of life in Lucknow. As a scholar of urban anthropology, he appreciated the efforts made by those in different parts of the world to coexist with people, religions, and cultures different from their own.

On the way to and from his home, Dr Ansari enjoyed walking past Turkish food stalls that sold halal meat. Other stalls sold pork-based food like sausages, salami, and bacon. There were also boisterous bars run by Serbian immigrants. He loved to tarry a while at the many open-air eateries overflowing with merrymakers from unknown backgrounds on balmy summer evenings.

For the same reason, he made a second home in Calpe. Dr Ansari had learnt from his time in Lucknow that diversity is the spice of life. He was happy that the Romans had discovered Calpe and catapulted the humble hamlet of fishermen and their art of drying and salting fish into a booming business. Apart from the sun-kissed weather and the breathtakingly beautiful beaches in Calpe, the Ansaris enjoyed looking up the history of various places. They visited architectural sights, hunted out the story of the origin of their favourite meals and tried to recognize vocabulary in the local Spanish language that had roots in another language spoken in a different corner of the planet. After all, Calpe had been, for the longest time the home of people from different civilizations, including Celts, Iberians, Greeks, Romans, and Muslims, making life there very similar to that in Lucknow.

A great cook, Dr Wadia made mouth-watering meals from the Middle East and loved to recall her first meeting with Dr Ansari in London. She had been a student of Arabic literature at the University of London, and after completing her studies, they had married and taught at different universities in Baghdad, Kuwait, Libya, and Vienna.

I learnt more about Firangi Mahal from Dr Ansari than during my days in Lucknow. Dr Ansari was amused to be served Lakhnawi korma, phulka, and yakhni pulao from my kitchen. He loved to talk in Urdu and said that childhood experiences of class differences in a seminary in Lucknow had disturbed him. There were fifteen boys in the class from families following different professions. Babu, the grandson of the household help, was in the same class. Because he was a Bhangi and belonged to the scavenger community, he was made to sit outside the classroom where upper-caste students left their shoes. Babu was allowed to repeat spellings and words recited from the Quran by the teacher, but he was not allowed to hold the holy book in his hand, lest the divine verses got polluted.

The thought of Babu made him pensive but he was also happy to use his example as the foundation of his academic research. As a child, it was difficult for him to deal with contradictions between the absolute egalitarian values taught by Islam and the caste discrimination practised by Muslims. Ideas of equality amongst mankind, universal brotherhood, and social justice had attracted him first to the Congress party in India, and later to Communism. He regretted that creative thinking was no longer the cornerstone of the Firangi Mahal milieu. The intellectually stifling atmosphere in the conservative environs of Firangi Mahal had made him flee Lucknow but memories of his childhood were still pleasant. With childlike glee, he recalled a ride on a rented bicycle to an industrial exhibition held by the British in an open area called Company Garden. The place is near the Firangi Mahal. He was about seven years old when the stalls full of English goods at the exhibition had made him determined to visit England one day.

Dr Ansari passed away in Vienna in 2012, the year I returned to make a home once again in Lucknow. I had spent three decades in Europe. When I visited Vienna recently, I talked to Dr Wadia on the phone. Although it is too exhausting for her to receive visitors now, she continues to live in Vienna, in the same place, on the same street in Ottakringer where the Turks and

a shadow of the past

the Slavs live sometimes in peace, and at other times, in disharmony. Dr Wadia asked about Khushwant Singh. I told her that he was no more. She remembered Khushwant Singh because it was Dr Ansari's desire that the popular journalist and bestselling author be entrusted with the task of translating *Umre Rafta*, his autobiography into English.

In 2002, Dr Ansari had published his two-volume autobiography, *Umre Rafta*, in Urdu. I had been given copies of both volumes for Khushwant Singh, with a request to translate Ansari's story. I did so, but never heard anything from Khushwant Singh who was about ninety years old at that time, but was still writing regularly.

In January 2017, I visited Bhopal and accompanied a friend to a local journalist's home for lunch. On the centre table of the living room I saw a book titled *The Transience of Life: A Memoir* by Ghaus Ansari. This was the translation of the first volume of *Umre Rafta* into English by Arif Ansari, his nephew.

That afternoon, I got to wondering why human beings bother to look for roots. I was reminded of the writings of Amin Maalouf, an Arab journalist from Beirut, living in exile in France and writing in French. He asks if human beings are trees that they should have roots. Human beings have legs and it is only natural for legs to wander around. That is why humanity has been moving from place to place for millions of years, without beginning and, perhaps, with no end.

That is why eighty-one-year-old Syed Abbas Jafar is still on the move. He is a glowing example of a Lucknow-born individual who no longer lives here but cannot resist visiting the city whenever he can. He lives in Bangalore and comes to Lucknow at least twice a year. Once in Lucknow, he travels further into the countryside to Kalanpur, his ancestral village in Jaunpur district. In Kalanpur he had inherited a corner of his parent's home that was rebuilt by him and fitted with modern-day amenities like a gas stove and a modern toilet. Every year during Muharram, the first month of the Islamic calendar, Jafar spends a week or so in Kalanpur. He catches up with old friends and relatives. He spends time in the village inhaling fresh air and taking long walks along crop-laden fields. He sits beside the pond, like he had as a child, to float clay lamps lit up with cotton wicks dipped in ghee. He attends the ritual majlis, the congregation of mostly Shia Muslims who collectively mourn the martyrdom (in 680 CE) of Imam Hussain, the revolutionary grandson of Prophet Muhammad.

This time of the year also serves as an occasion for relatives scattered all over the country to meet each other once again in the ancestral village. Jafar enjoys the special meals served during Muharram that bring back memories of his late mother. After this hectic interaction with an entire community of people he has known since childhood, Jafar returns to Bangalore, rejuvenated. That Jafar's trips to Lucknow include Kalanpur is only natural. For this is the continuation of the tradition of land-owning and socially significant families who maintained dual homes—in rural and urban areas.

As an imperial capital, Lucknow had kept itself closely connected with the countryside, the source of its wealth. Important administrators in urban areas had roots in the countryside where the qasba enjoyed a rich cultural life for almost 200 years. In Arabic, al-Casbah means the citadel and hub of medieval towns. However, qasba here implies a neighbourhood of wealthy, landowning families, situated between a village and a city, and dotted with temples, mosques, and shrines. Unlike in a village, the landowners in a qasba lived in sprawling mansions fenced in by walled gardens and groves made secure with tall gates. The many qasbas in the region were centres of rural power. They were also home to universities of learning and piety.

Kalanpur is about 350 kilometres away from Lucknow and is home to a close-knit community of Shia Muslims. Here, the way of life is similar to that of a qasba in close proximity to the capital city. Kalanpur is also the ancestral village of Sir Syed Wazir Hasan, jurist and politician, and one of the five brothers of Jafar's paternal grandfather. The agricultural land owned by Hasan's family in the heartland of the Indo–Gangetic plain was probably gifted to his ancestors of Persian origin by a Mughal emperor pleased with their heroics on the battlefield.

Once soldiers became landlords, they gave up

fighting to settle down to the more sedentary life of a farmer. With time, agricultural land got divided into smaller and smaller fields amongst the many descendants of the landlord, forcing some to move to urban areas in search of alternative ways to make a living. Hasan was one of the first young men to leave the village of Kalanpur in the early twentieth century to study law in the city and to be rewarded with the job of a jurist.

As secretary and, later, president of the All India Muslim League, Hasan was a champion of rapprochement between the Indian National Congress and the Muslim League. He was responsible for transforming Muslim League politics to bring it closer to the Congress. He drafted a new constitution for the Muslim League, allowing it to work with other concerned citizens for a system of self-government suitable for all Indians. As a leading lawyer of his generation, Hasan had the backing of landlords with small landholdings. His young party within the Muslim League had distanced itself from the old party of large landholders and successful men whose interests were often tied to those of the British. Hasan's group of politicians stood for a united India and opposed the idea of Pakistan. The group had its fair share of critics and some saw it as the source of all evil, and dangerous and ruinous to the cause of Islam. Hasan and his followers were famous as the Lucknow Gang that made the pact between the Congress and the Muslim League possible in 1916. After the Lucknow Pact was signed, the focus of

a shadow of the past

Indian politics gradually moved away from the coastal cities of Mumbai and Kolkata towards the heartland.

Hasan had turned his back on agriculture and a rustic life in the countryside to become the first Indian chief justice of the Awadh Court, and, later, president of the Muslim League. For many relatives who wanted to migrate from the village to the city after him, Hasan was a mentor and a guardian.

That is how Jafar's father got the courage to move out of the village of Kalanpur. Hasan, an influential figure, was a paternal uncle and helped him to find a government job. After retirement, Jafar's parents settled down in Lucknow. Jafar has a postgraduate degree in geology from Lucknow University. His first assignment abroad was with the Geological Survey of Austria, where he learnt the German language. He returned to a teaching job at the Aligarh Muslim University and, later, taught at Germany's University of Tubingen. He retired about two decades ago from Lucknow's Birbal Sahni Institute of Palaeobotany, and because his wife is from Hyderabad, they decided to live in South India. He continues to travel around the world but returns to Lucknow for yet another plate of toor dal, garnished with chopped garlic fried in ghee. This dish is made this way only in Lucknow.

A few years ago, Jafar concluded that the journey from Bangalore to Lucknow and then to Kalanpur was exhausting. So he sold his property in the village and now restricts his visits to Lucknow. Ask Jafar why he bothers to come here, and without blinking an eye, he replies that when he is not in Lucknow his ears crave the sound of the Urdu language. When that desire becomes impossible to bear, Jafar returns to the city of perfumed eloquence just for a chit-chat with the people in Lucknow.

Numerous Lakhnauwalas like Jafar scattered around the world believe that circumstances may have separated Lucknow from them but that it is impossible to separate them from Lucknow. They find magic in the city. The Shaam-e-Awadh evenings, when the skies are clothed in shocking pink, are full of wonder. At sunset, as I have noted earlier the tradition is for citizens to emerge from their homes to indulge in 'ganjing' and to enjoy the gentle breeze from the Gomti in the company of friends. This breeze is responsible for inspiring so many of the city's citizens to write and appreciate poetry. Locally, the balmy breeze is called purvaiya. On this side of the river, people wait for the purvaiya to arrive and to smooth away sweat from the brows of citizens after sunset. The coming of the purvaiya heralds the promise of relief from the sweltering heat that keeps the Indo–Gangetic plain in its grip for a large part of the day. The purvaiya is said to seduce the aesthetic sensibility of the city by overpowering the hearts and minds of the citizens with local fragrances like khus, mitti, rose, and jasmine. The colourful sunset, river, breeze, aroma of flowers, mingled with the preparation of evening meals, and the sound of anklets in the shadow of candlelight, all contribute to that experience called Shaam-e-Awadh. The seductively swaying purvaiya remains a favourite muse of poets, both classical and popular.

Writes Anand Bakshi for a 1975 Hindi film:

> Silently sings the purvaiya
> look at him on the flute,
> and the belles
> frolic with kanhaiya!

Iftikhar Arif was born in Lucknow in 1943. In 1965, he migrated to Pakistan where he enjoyed a glorious career in radio and television. He is also celebrated as one of the most romantic Urdu poets in contemporary times. After his first poetry collection won him instant recognition three decades ago, he decided to do nothing else in life except write poetry. He compares his compulsion to compose verse to that of the nightingale's obsession to sing till it drops dead.

Iftikhar traces his relationship to poetry to the air he inhaled in the city of his birth. Wherever he looked, he found poetry in Lucknow. Once he had navigated the winding streets in the old city of Lucknow with his eyes closed. Today those streets are mapped on his heart. His memories of Shaam-e-Awadh include strains of Bekal Utsahi's poetry recited in the local dialect of Awadhi. Iftikhar remembers walking along the Gomti at sunset, mesmerized by the purple and pink skyline of the city. Once in a while, he would take a boat ride on the river and, inspired by the ambience around him, would burst into song even in his unmelodious voice. In Lucknow, Iftikhar was addicted to watching the sun disappear every evening behind the many domes and minarets of mosques, temples, and shrines. He waited breathlessly for the night, darker than kohl, to be illuminated lamp by lamp. This ritual by the rich and the poor alike took place every evening to the sound of temple bells, bhajans, and hymns sung publicly in praise of Prophet Muhammad. The jingling of the ghungroo, and many a beat tapped upon the tabla, were the essential notes of the Shaam-e-Awadh orchestra. It still thrills him to recall the daily preparations that would take place for a night-long congregation of poets, all in anticipation of a rendezvous between beauty and love.

Professionally, the migration did him good, but the loneliness that he suffers even today often makes him want to die. Iftikhar continues to write mostly about love, longing, loneliness, and learning. Today, his verses are an inspiration for many contemporary Urdu poets in Lucknow, like Abhishek Shukla.

Abhishek, who was born in 1985, sometimes talks to Iftikhar on the phone. Abhishek told me that listening to Iftikhar is like flipping through the pages of a beautiful book on life. Every word that the older poet says to him is a lesson.

Thirty-four-year-old Himanshu Bajpai, writer and storyteller, adds that Iftikhar may have countless fans around the world but he considers himself the poet's most ardent fan. Himanshu lives in a neighbourhood

a shadow of the past

close to where Iftikhar lived more than five decades ago. It is easy for Himanshu to identify with the beauty, intensity, and sobriety found in the poetry of Iftikhar, and with the poet's recitation of verses in classical Urdu, still spoken in the older parts of the city. Himanshu told me that Iftikhar's poetry awakens different aspects of Lucknow that lie asleep in his soul.

FOUR

The Honey-Tongued

The world swoons when a Lakhnauwala speaks in a language that sounds as if it is dipped in honey. The gift of the gab of even those on the street is such that the presence of a beloved is routinely described as a fragrance, and the utterance of lovers is praised as Urdu. Over time, a certain mystique became associated with Urdu because it seemed to have the power to throw light on the yet undiscovered secrets of love and life. Look at how gloom is imagined in Urdu. It is compared to the inability of the pen to document pain because the hand is glued to the chest, nursing a broken heart. Urdu poetry describes bliss as that moment when the beloved is finally face-to-face with the lover. And the poet thinks it worthwhile to spend an entire lifetime in anticipation of this magical moment.

The Urdu language was not always as sophisticated as it eventually evolved to be. This love child of classical Farsi, local Indian dialects, and Sanskrit literary traditions has humble origins. The seed of Urdu took root with the subcontinent's first rendezvous with Arabs who visited much before the advent of Islam.

a shadow of the past

Attempts by seafaring traders, merchants on foot, and on horseback to communicate with each other is how Urdu was born. The word Urdu is derived from a Turkic word meaning both army and encampment.

Urdu thrived in Lucknow mostly amongst Farsi-speaking Turkic, Mongol, and Persian scholars, traders, and warriors. It took time for the language to flower into literature, which it did mainly through poets and wandering mystics, both Hindu and Muslim. The minstrels traversed the subcontinent constantly, resting for a while in one place and disappearing before the sun came up. Their songs about unity between the Creator and the many creatures of the world were composed in vocabulary picked up during their travels and were so beautiful that the crowds did not tire of listening to them. Their songs were mostly about love, equality of all human beings, and religious tolerance.

Since the twelfth century, Urdu has enriched itself by borrowing words from every Indian language that crossed its path as it loafed around South Asia for almost half a millennium. From Gulbarga, Bijapur, and Golkonda in the south, to Gujarat in the west, when Urdu returned to Delhi, it was already armed with an incredible vocabulary. The language picked up new words every day but its grammar remained the same as the local language. That made Urdu understood and loved by all the different people it met during a lifetime spent on the road. It was able to give interesting twists to ideas through the colloquial vocabulary at its command. Mystic poet Wali Muhammad Deccani was born in Maharashtra and buried in Gujarat. He visited Delhi in 1700 and wowed the literati in the imperial capital with love songs called ghazals that used unusual combinations of words from Farsi and local languages. Wali's straightforward but sensuous language forced the pompous intelligentsia that had so far worked only in Farsi to acknowledge that Urdu was good enough to be used before the king.

By the time it settled down in Lucknow around the middle of the eighteenth century, Urdu was laced with enticing idioms gifted to the language by dialects of Sirhindi, Braj Bhasha, Khari Boli, and Hindawi. Urdu pleased everyone, as listeners recognized many words borrowed from their mother tongues. Urdu was popular as it shared philosophical ideas in a language understood by ordinary citizens.

Insha Allah Khan Insha, a Lucknow poet of the early nineteenth century, formalized the grammar of the Urdu language and used it to praise Lord Krishna. Insha says that the image of the dark-skinned torso of Krishna draped in a mustard shawl makes him dizzy with want. Almost a century later, Arzoo Lakhnavi continued, as if in the same breath: 'veiled like a dream comes the enlightened one to wake up those still asleep'.

Hasrat Mohani, progressive poet of the twentieth century, travelled to Mecca eleven times and made a pilgrimage to Mathura, Krishna's place of birth, an equal number of times. In every mosque or temple

a shadow of the past

that he visited, he saw the beauty of his beloved. The poet felt that it was Krishna's look, so full of love, that had showed him the way to Mathura. But, once in Mathura, he was filled with doubt and wondered whether his beloved would accept his love or not.

Mohani coined the slogan 'Inquilab Zindabad' (long live the revolution) for the Indian freedom movement. When he was not standing up to the British, the poet concentrated on adoring Krishna, a symbol of never-ending love. To the utter joy of the man on the street, Mohani praised Krishna in simple vocabulary borrowed from local dialects spoken in the rural areas surrounding Lucknow. In Mohani's verse, the poet assumes the persona of the female aashiq or lover who spends an entire life expressing unconditional ishq or love for the mashooq, the beloved.

In Mathura, Mohani fell in love with the flute, Krishna's favourite musical instrument. The sound overwhelmed his heart and in the music of the flute he heard a call for unity amongst all creatures on earth. 'Hasrat, you are fortunate in your love for the one whose complexion is darker than the colour of musk,' wrote Mohani. After every trip to Mathura, Mohani came away assured that the only job of human beings is to care for each other and that this is the only truth worth living for.

Urdu poets keep trying to make poetry lovers fall in love with the idea of love—the kind of love that transcends caste, class, and religious divides. This is best reflected in the writing of Brij Narayan Chakbast, a Kashmiri Pandit lawyer who wrote in Urdu in the first quarter of the twentieth century. From his home in Qaiserbagh, he said that it is impossible to experience joy without knowing pain. The poet warns human beings that they will be deprived of enjoying life if they refuse to love out of fear of being hurt.

After his death in 1926, it became increasingly difficult for his family to take care of the sprawling Chakbast home in the colonial-style Qaiserbagh complex. Squatters took advantage and moved into the premises. The colonial style kothi was recently demolished, much to the consternation of heritage lovers who helplessly watched as another chapter of the city's past disappeared into dust, despite the cries of the poet that sounds may die but that which strikes the eye lives long in the mind.

Over the decades, many architectural beauties have been lost, slowly destroying Lucknow's reputation as a place of great wonder and extravagance.

Of course, the wasteful frivolity of nineteenth-century Lucknow had to go along with feudal ways of the court. The regret is not to have prepared Lucknow to face contemporary challenges gracefully. It seems to be forgotten that at one time, other capitals like Delhi and Lahore were dwarfed by the elegance of commercial and cultural activities in Lucknow. A city that was once the envy of medieval monarchs has been reduced to one of the most backward and poverty-stricken places in the country.

a shadow of the past

That is why Maxine Reding (nee Cline) from Adelaide, Australia, has difficulty in recognizing Lucknow. She left the city nearly half a century ago. Maxine was born in Lucknow to Anglo–Indian parents, and spent the first sixteen years of her life in the city. In all these decades, the retired linguist and educationist did not forget what a wealthy confluence of vocabularies Urdu is. Recently, she forwarded a message on WhatsApp, announcing her visit to Lucknow and to say how much she looked forward to a goshti (high tea) such as she had enjoyed in the past. As she planned the trip to Lucknow in September 2018 to coincide with a reunion of the alumni of the La Martinière College, Urdu tumbled out of her memory like a waterfall. She remembered her mother, Cynthia, preparing high tea for friends in their Lucknow home. The gathering was called goshti, the Sanskrit word for conversation. The youngest of three children of Archie and Cynthia Cline, Maxine and her family of European origin spoke fluent Urdu while in Lucknow. Cynthia gave birth to Maxine in the chaupar colony, the old Lawrence Terrace built in the shape of a cross in the nineteenth century as a stable for the royalty. Once the monarchy ended in Lucknow, the chaupar complex was taken over by the British and named Lawrence Terrace after Brigadier General Sir Henry Lawrence, the Resident representing the East India Company in Lucknow, who was killed in the 1857 war. The stables were converted into homes for Anglo-Indian families, an entire community born of mixed parentage of European men and Indian women. Once they became rulers of the country, the British frowned upon marriages with Indians. Shiploads of women arrived from England, instead, to wed Englishmen in India. The Anglo-Indians saw themselves as European people born in India and who were trusted by the British administration. They were given plum jobs in the railways, post and telegraph services, and the armed forces. Most of the staff in numerous schools, colleges, and hospitals, that were funded by the British, were also of European descent. The British had won the war in Lucknow in 1857 against the local population. Wajid Ali Shah, the last monarch had already surrendered his crown in 1856 and had left Lucknow to make a home in Kolkata. After nearly a year of warring, the rebellious citizens lost Lucknow to the British. The new masters turned their nose up at Chowk and other parts of the old city with their mysterious lanes and narrow alleys. They tore them down to build a modern, colonial metropolis with broad, straight roads and large pavements. A Big Ben lookalike clock tower came up just opposite the eighteenth-century Imambara complex built by Asaf-ud-Daula, Lucknow's first ruler. Single-storey bungalows were built for British officials. A cantonment for hectic military activities came up, after destroying dozens of villages. A magnificent club was designed for soldiers where the white nawabs could chill at the bar, play billiards and pool. In the late nineteenth century, Lucknow was a cosmopolitan city attracting

Parsi liquor barons and Bania businessmen, including numerous moneylenders and jewellers. Newal Kishore came to Lucknow all the way from Lahore to open Asia's first printing press that did roaring business, publishing textbooks for government schools. Hotels mushroomed everywhere in the city, more luxurious than the Carlton and The Savoy in London. Hospitals and shopping centres multiplied, making Lucknow a seat of learning and worship, as missionaries built several churches and schools. By the end of the nineteenth century, Lucknow was converted into a very Anglo-Indian city, that was made safe, orderly, and clean for nearly 5,000 British soldiers and civilians to inhabit. Maxine had lived in Lawrence Terrace along with Rover, her dog, and Timothy, her parrot, till October 1968. After that, the family migrated to Australia.

'We enjoyed such a wide cultural experience growing up in Lawrence Terrace and were brought up to respect them all. When I relate stories of how I had celebrated Holi, Diwali, Eid, Muharram and, of course, Easter and Christmas in Lawrence Terrace to my husband, children, and friends, they think I am making them up. Even the truth that I was born in old Lawrence Terrace, the chaupar, where the royalty kept elephants and horses is still met with raised eyebrows, especially at Christmas time. The lead-up to festivities like making wicks for diyas with Aunty Nehru Srivastava, chopping dried fruits for Christmas cakes while sneaking pinches of it into the mouth are memories still steadfast in my brain.'

Back in Lucknow in 2018, Maxine wondered why the annual fair on the sprawling grounds of the Shah Najaf Imambara was no longer held. Built on the banks of the Gomti in the early nineteenth century by another Shia Muslim ruler of Lucknow of Persian origin, the Shah Najaf is a replica of the tomb of Ali in the Iraqi city of Najaf and sacred, especially to Shia Muslims. Ali was a close companion, cousin, and son-in-law of Muhammad, the Prophet of Islam, and a great hero in the eyes of Shia Muslims. These details about the Shah Najaf were of little interest to Maxine who recalled enjoying the fair with her parents and siblings, and looked forward to feasting on the halwa parantha sold there. Maxine burst into tears when she stood outside her home in Lawrence Terrace to discover that it has been turned into a neon-light-decorated cloth shop that also sells saris!

In Australia, Maxine nurses this nostalgia by recreating meals that were prepared by Changga, the khansama with six fingers, who was employed by her parents as a chef in their Lawrence Terrace home. But the taste is never the same. Her mother, Cynthia, who had been totally dependent upon Changga to feed the family in Lucknow, took a few years to become quite a khansamin in Australia, says Maxine. Maxine remembers all her friends from Lawrence Terrace and from La Martinière College. Their cultural and religious backgrounds were but this did not come in the way of friendship. She keeps in touch with many of them and is grateful to Lucknow for having taught her so early in life to be friends with all human beings without reserve, a lesson that helped her to feel at home in Australia sooner than she thought.

Archie Cline, Maxine's father, was brought up in Bangalore and employed by the British Indian Army to keep hundreds of vehicles used by the military in working order. Lucknow was the home of the Northern Command of the army and, during World War II, Archie was called up north to take care of the motor-vehicle business here. It is in Lucknow that he met Cynthia and fell in love with her; he stayed on to make a home with her and to eat curry with a spoon. Life was good for this community for nearly a century; the years after 1947 were, however, difficult. Anglo-Indian families found themselves caught between two worlds. They were Indian but also felt orphaned after the British left the country. Many were unsure of where they wanted to live.

Years were spent wondering whether to leave the country or to stay. Some Anglo-Indian families followed the British to Great Britain, reducing their population in the country from half a million in 1947 to less than 150,000 today. The Clines did not migrate immediately after the British left, as business was good at the Bombay Garage that Archie owned in Lucknow. Cynthia was happy with her job at Lucknow's Literacy House. After the British left, however, the government contract to maintain vehicles was not renewed. But Archie continued to earn good money by taking care of vintage cars owned by affluent landlords and members of the business community.

With the British gone, a feeling of insecurity crept into the lives of Anglo-Indians who worried that the local people would turn against them. The community had thrived under the British despite the fact that Anglo-Indians were dismissed as brown, undesirable, and alien by way of the white rulers. The British saw Anglo-Indians as black, while the Anglo-Indians thought of themselves as white and, therefore, superior to Indians. As their number decreased, their plight worsened. Khushwant Singh once said that the tragedy of the Anglo-Indians was largely of their own making. 'Begging to be accepted as white, they minimized or even denied their Indianness. Thus, the Indians soon came to despise them. And the whites treated them with contempt....' That is why many Anglo-Indians were unsure if they would be accepted in Britain.

Mauveen Shaw, educationist, went through a rough patch in the 1960s when there was a lot of discrimination against descendants of the British in Lucknow. All Anglo-Indian girls of her generation had grown up wearing western dresses but, after a while, people would taunt Mauveen saying, 'Haven't the English left yet?'

It had depressed her to hear that, so, after a while, Mauveen took to wearing only salwar-kameez and other traditional Indian dresses. She laughs now to see so many young girls wearing shorts and spaghetti-strap tops while she loves wearing saris. The departure of most Anglo-Indians and the assimilation of others also spelt the end of chic restaurants in Lucknow. People would go to these eateries to listen to a live band and to dance on a wooden floor after a hearty meal of jalfrezi, meatball curry, roast beef, vegetarian and non-vegetarian cutlets, and lip-smacking puddings. The annual May Queen Ball and New Year's Eve Ball as hosted by the British have been wiped out even from the memory of a past that becomes hazier with each passing day.

Today, the Anglo-Indians in the city find it difficult to renew the lease of their homes, reducing the community to a state of neglect. Anglo-Indians often complain of being terrorized by thugs who threaten to demolish graveyards and obelisks. However, community members are also determined to exercise their right to live in the city as equal citizens of the country and to safeguard their dignity. Adrian Michael, head of the Lucknow branch of the All India Anglo-Indian Association, counts 310 members today. This is good news for the association that was founded in 1876 to safeguard the charitable, cultural, and educational interests of the community but was declared defunct in 2014 due to the non-payment of dues by its members. Adrian says that the revived organization also serves as a platform for entrepreneurial ventures. The monthly meets these days encourage the display of cuisine, wines, pickles, and cakes in an effort to preserve the Anglo-Indian way of life. Non-Anglo-Indians are not invited to the meet in order to maintain the exclusive ethos of the community that perceives itself as a linguistic minority aiming to safeguard its values and culture. The events are hosted by Carlyle McFarland, headmaster of La Martinière Boys College. Despite the challenges faced by Anglo-Indians, McFarland has no regrets about staying back in the city where he was born. McFarland is one of the most admired citizens of Lucknow today as an educationist. The city is proud of McFarland for helping to restore the 175-year-old Constantia, now the prestigious La Martinière College, with financial help from ex-students. McFarland keeps the doors of Constantia open, and visitors are encouraged to visit the campus and witness the restoration work done under the supervision of Ansar-ud-din, a local master craftsman.

In the late nineteenth century, Constantia was built as a home for Major General Claude Martin. However before he could move into his dream home, he died. In his treasury, Martin left several million pounds, which he said should be used to educate Anglo-Indian students. After Independence, Indians were allowed admission to the school and, today, the campus tutors around 4,000 children. Martin was a remarkable man who was born in Lyons, France, in 1735 and died in Lucknow in 1800.

In a 1796 letter to a European friend, Martin wrote that he had begun building a house and visiting the site every morning on horseback and every afternoon in a carriage. He felt that spending time on the site, even building the house, would improve his health as he would be away from the city.

In 1840, the magnificent Constantia, spread over an area of about 350 acres, opened as La Martinière College for Boys. However, over time, it suffered neglect and wore a look as forlorn as the future of Anglo-Indians in the city. That is, until McFarland took over as principal in 2010. That same year, he met master craftsman Ansar-ud-din whose wizardry exposed and enhanced the original Plaster of Paris Wedgwood designs. The eighteenth-century English potter Josiah Wedgwood is believed to have made the Plaster of Paris plaques in the library and in the chapel at La Martinière College. The rendering of Apollo and Nine Muses seen in one room are similar to the original Wedgwood designs on the jasper urns now on display at London's Victoria and Albert Museum. This room serves as a study for senior resident scholars on campus. Every ceiling is unique with decorations in bas reliefs, arabesques, and other ornamentation. When the French authorities heard of this building, they came to see it and the French government awarded a medal of honour to Ansar-ud-din and his team of fifteen artisans. The French authorities are delighted to see that it is a living building and have included it in a list of French monuments outside of France.

McFarland is happy to be here today and feels

that he would not be accepted in any other European country in the same way as he is accepted in India. He clearly feels as Indian as the Ganga, but is also proud of his unique Anglo-Indian ancestry.

McFarland sees himself as a linguistic minority whose first language is English. He grew up listening to the BBC on an old Murphy Radio that he still keeps in his office. His paternal ancestors came from Scotland. An ancestor found employment in the British East India Company in Kolkata in an apothecary of the British Indian Army. Later, the McFarlands moved north as employees of the Northern Railways, and eventually settled down in Lucknow. McFarland remembers the conversations he had with the late Frank Anthony, once the nominated representative of Anglo-Indians in the Indian parliament. Anthony was known as the leading light of the community and embraced local ways after 1947. He did not miss an opportunity to remind his community to come out of their shells, open up to other Indians, and learn Hindi. Anthony taught himself to enjoy local food like biryani, kebabs, and aloo tikki because he felt that eating together brings people closer.

Joan Yeoward, an alumnus of La Martinière Girls College was blond, with waist-length hair, and blue eyes. In the 1970s, she was often confronted by the police and asked to prove her identity. Only after Joan proved that she was Indian and not a hippie was she left alone. Apart from English, Joan also speaks the local dialect of the people living in the countryside around

a shadow of the past

Gonda district, some 120 kilometres from Lucknow. Today one of the most backward areas of Uttar Pradesh, Gonda was once the centre of agricultural activities. Several sugar mills and rice mills are still to be found in the area. Joan's ancestors received agricultural land in Gonda from the British. Her father and uncles were employees of the Northern Railways.

'All my aunts who married men from outside Gonda have migrated. My parents and my siblings love our village and the people here too much to leave. Not once have I thought of migrating to live anywhere else in the world,' says Joan, who retired as a welfare officer with the Northern Indian Railways. She leads a quiet life in Gonda now, dyes her hair black, and wears saris and salwar kurtas. Joan believes that the Ganga-Jamuni way of life is not only about Hindu and Muslim cultures flowing into each other. The confluence is also enriched by countless ideas pooled in by lesser-known people and cultures like the many tributaries of the great rivers.

FIVE

Mad About Movies

Veena Talwar Oldenburg, a Lakhnawi, who taught History at Baruch College and the Graduate Center of the University of New York, agrees that life in her hometown is a colourful mosaic of many different cultures. The mosaic includes dollops of the Dravidian, Central Asian, and European ways of life that thrived when it was encouraged by well-meaning community leaders who wanted to make living here an experience closest to paradise.

The latest addition to the mosaic that is Lucknow is Sandeep Kumar. I first met Sandeep in the Austrian capital, Vienna. Sandeep is a Punjabi who studied marketing in Germany. He is now an Austrian citizen and, in 2008, when I met him in a multiplex cinema hall in Vienna, he was working for a multinational company. What I share in common with Sandeep is a love for films. While in Vienna, I witnessed him shoot his first experimental film with an interesting Indo-Austrian plot and cast. The awards and bouquets that he received for this venture inspired him to give up his office job as a marketing professional to make movies. I remember

a shadow of the past

giving the muhurat shot for his second film before I left Vienna in 2012. Vienna had been my home for three decades and I was happy to be back in Lucknow to make a new home here.

Sandeep visited my new home in Lucknow soon enough. Within three days of his stay here, he had fallen in love with the city. He was amazed at the exquisite embroidery on muslin cloth and found it difficult to choose something for his mother. Continuing to rejoice in the mild sunshine on a beautiful October day and in the midst of many a mouthful of tangy street food, Sandeep promised to make his next film in Lucknow. Sandeep was also attracted to Lucknow because it is the home of actor Farrukh Jaffar. He was already familiar with her work as the bed-ridden but boisterous amma in Anusha Rizvi's award-winning 2010 film, *Peepli Live*. He remembered her as Rekha's mother in *Umrao Jaan* (1981) and was overjoyed to find himself in the same room with the octogenarian female actor, also famous for fatwa on her index finger, and films on her mind. She is the inspiration for Tamboli Begum, an indomitable character in my last book, *Love and Life in Lucknow*. Her claim to fame is her work with the three big Khans of Indian cinema. She was seen with Shah Rukh Khan in *Swades* (2004), Salman Khan in *Sultan* (2016) and Aamir Khan in *Secret Superstar* (2017). After many hours of a heart-to-heart with the actor, Sandeep returned to Vienna. Within weeks, I heard that he had come up with a story about an amazing senior citizen in Lucknow who led life on her own terms. He made a life-size poster announcing Farrukh Jaffar in and as *Mehrunisa,* a very Lakhnawi title with a Persian flavour. In Farsi, 'mah' means moon, and 'nisa' means woman—together, Mehrunisa means a woman with a face as beautiful as the moon.

When Sandeep met Farrukh Jaffar, she was eighty-six years old. She had enacted numerous roles—sister, mother, and grandmother—on screen for almost half a century. Now, she was flattered to play the lead character in *Mehrunisa.* Sandeep was ecstatic over the partnership. He was back in Lucknow to set up a team and to shoot the film in the autumn of 2018.

While planning the filming of *Mehrunisa,* Sandeep also met vocalist Sunita Jhingran Sharma. The saffron-clad Sunita is claustrophobic. So, she could not use the escalator in Sandeep's apartment and walked up ten floors to meet him. Once she got back her breath, this devotee of Hanuman introduced herself to the Punjabi boy with an Austrian passport as a slave of the hero of Karbala.

Sunita sang for Sandeep. She chose verses about the tranquillity that human beings experience once they fall in love with the Creator of the universe. This is one relationship, between the Creator and his creation, that is free of jealousy and free from fears of infidelity, sang Sunita.

Sandeep did not understand much of what she said, but he was floored. And the less he understood what

Sunita said to him the more he was attracted to her. The eclectic Sunita told Sandeep that she is a Hussaini Brahmin. She traced her ancestry to Rahab Sidh Dutt of the Mohyal clan of career soldiers. Sunita took him back to pre-Islamic Arabia where some Mohyals had lived with scores of other Hindu families, engaged mostly in trade. In the seventh century, Rahab was friends with Imam Hussain, younger grandson of Muhammad, the Prophet of Islam. In 680 CE, when Hussain faced the army of a cruel dictator on a battlefield beside the Euphrates, Rahab and his sons fought beside him. They lost the battle and, along with the followers of Hussain, Rahab's family continues to mourn his martyrdom. The non-Muslim devotees of Hussain from the family of Rahab are called Hussaini Brahmins. And Ali, the father of Hussain and closest companion of the Prophet, is often evoked by Hussaini Brahmins as Om Murti.

Unlike Muslim devotees who wear black clothes during the mourning period of Muharram, Sunita continues to don a saffron sari. The saffron colour is sacred to Hindus and symbolizes one's personal quest for truth. The maternal side of Sunita's family goes back to Tansen, the musical wizard in the court of Emperor Akbar. Music is in her blood and Sunita seldom needs an invitation to sing.

Born in the crowded part of the old city of Lucknow, Sunita was four years old when her father introduced her to Sanskrit verses that she memorized. She is trained in North Indian classical music and feels fortunate to have received lessons in the art of folk singing from the legendary ghazal singer, the late Begum Akhtar, who sang songs of love in a voice sweeter than that of a nightingale. Born Akhtari, into a family of traditional courtesans from Faizabad, she was gifted the title of Begum after she married a leading lawyer in Lucknow. She lived in the city till her death in 1974.

Sunita spent her childhood in the Shia Muslim neighbourhood of Sheesh Mahal. This place was once a glittering quarter of Daulat Khana, Asaf-ud-Daula's palace complex on the banks of the river in the Husainabad area. Sheesh Mahal was Lucknow's first palace city. Later rulers moved to the Chattar Manzil and Qaiserbagh. The medieval Husainabad complex reflects only a faint whiff of its former grandeur but it is still a sight to behold. The premises of the Daulat Khana are populated by the many descendants of the former royal family who continue to practice a Shia Muslim way of life. Sunita recalls that the ambience of the neighbourhood left a deep impression on her. As a child, she would participate in the different rituals observed throughout the year by her Muslim neighbours. She was about ten years old when she was introduced to the writings of the nineteenth-century Urdu poet Mir Babbar Ali Anees, who has narrated the martyrdom of Hussain at Karbala in a long poem. This type of elegy is called marsiya, and the one by Anees is a glowing example of a historical narrative penned in pre-modern Urdu. The language is lyrical and the oral recitation of

a shadow of the past

the verses in the style of storytelling is most dramatic. The text is in sehal zabaan, easy language, making listeners feel as if characters in anguish from a bygone era are their own loved ones.

The poet says may God protect him from the evil eye; his eloquence touches the heart, although, for two long days, his throat is dry.

It was natural for him to emote the way he did, because Anees was born in a Shia Muslim family in Faizabad in 1802. He grew up in Lucknow, a city ruled by a Shia Muslim dynasty. It is clear from his poetry that Anees had deep knowledge of Arabic and Farsi. He was also familiar with the history and culture of the Arabs and the Persians, in particular, of historical events. The poet is admired for the wealth of vocabulary he used with ease in Urdu, Persian, and Arabic and for using many words from different languages with the same meaning in one line. This is a unique feature found in the work of many Lucknow poets.

Anees writes that here, amongst thorns, the Prophet's flowers provide fragrance to the desert land, as the house of Fatima faces its last hours in the garden planted by Muhammad's hand, the garden cut down in ten days by a cruel band.

The emotional outburst of Anees in his verses on Karbala resonated with the resentment people felt at the presence of the British in Lucknow. Wajid Ali Shah, the last ruler of Lucknow, had been forced to renounce the throne. Similarly, the tragedy faced by Hussain in

Karbala was unfair and unjust. A year after Wajid Ali Shah left for Kolkata, Lucknow was at war with the British. During the war, Anees fled Lucknow to camp with his family in the mango orchard of a friend in Malihabad, 30 kilometres away from Lucknow. For nearly a year he lived in a tent. Anees saw the takeover of Lucknow by the British as a tragedy on a par with the incident at Karbala. With the dismantling of the monarchy, Anees lost his income. He was forced to travel to Patna, Benaras, and Hyderabad to earn a living. Everywhere he went, a large crowd gathered to listen to him. In Hyderabad, no venue had seemed large enough to accommodate the audience. Even getting a place to stand was difficult to find when the magic of Anees was unleashed as he recited from the top of the pulpit, as if in a trance. After each trip, the poet always returned home to his beloved Lucknow where he died in 1874.

When Sunita was young, she liked to join the traditional congregation to listen to raconteurs repeat the story of the battle of Karbala. Master storytellers rendered the same incident in different styles of elegies and dirges like marsiya, soz, and noha.

Sunita's numerous recitations of her devotion to Hussain touched Sandeep. One day, he asked her if he could use her voice to strengthen the dramatic narrative of *Mehrunisa*. Sunita came up with five compositions for Sandeep that have been recorded without any musical accompaniment. Sunita's extremely spiritual and raw voice is haunting.

After auditions with the local talent, a team of cast and crew was put together for *Mehrunisa*. Christian Haake, German cinematographer, and Herbert Verdino, Austrian sound engineer, joined the crew of *Mehrunisa*. The buzz within the team of *Mehrunisa* reminded me of the excitement that the visit of the German painter Johan Zoffany, of Bohemian and Hungarian origin, must have caused in eighteenth-century Lucknow. There was also the French speaking, Swiss-born Antoine Polier who wandered into Lucknow in 1780 and realized the aesthetic and commercial benefits of staying on.

Writes Nasima Aziz in *Wandering in the Lanes of History 1700s and 1800s:*

> He (Polier) found the European community having almost daily interaction with the court, at lavish banquets or at performances staged for one purpose only, the entertainment of the guests…. He became part of a circle of expatriates like himself, living a life part western, part eastern, acquiring a huge collection of 17th and 18th century Persian, Arabic and Sanskrit manuscripts, Mughal miniatures, books and antiquities of all kinds.

The very ingenious Claude Martin had been in Lucknow since 1775. By the time he died in 1800, it was suspected that he was more affluent than the ruler. John Wombwell, the Company's accountant, wore local clothes and enjoyed many a drag on the hubble-bubble hookah. The promise of earning thousands of pounds had drawn painter Ozias Humphry to Lucknow. Humphry got the gregarious Asaf-ud-Daula to pose for him. Colonel John Mordaunt was head of the ruler's bodyguard and shared with Asaf-ud-Daula a love for cockfights.

Sophia Elizabeth Plowden, wife of one of the Nawab's bodyguards, spent time with the nautch girls in Lucknow. She was starstruck on meeting Khanum Jan, a celebrity courtesan of her time. Khanum Jan was a trained vocalist and her singing made the lyrical love poems of the fourteenth-century Persian poet, Hafiz Shirazi, hugely popular in Lucknow. Sophia had a beautiful voice and was a frequent visitor to the home of Khanum Jan. The enterprising woman collected lyrics from local singers, translated them into English and sang them to Indian tunes. On a harp gifted to her by Claude Martin, she created a new style of music called Hindustani Airs that became a craze in the shimmering, cosmopolitan city of Lucknow.

I have no idea what *Mehrunisa* will look like on screen. What I do know is that everyone who has worked with Sandeep salutes his passion for cinema. He has earned much goodwill in a city unfamiliar to him till a while ago. He is admired for his courage to cast an eighty-six-year-old female actor as the protagonist in a film that is also produced by him. I can only salaam the spirit of the strangers who keep appearing in the city in the hope of realizing their dreams.

SIX

The World is My Oyster

At the time of Partition, the population of Lucknow was half a million. Today, it has increased to nearly 3 million, but the economy has remained stagnant. Overpopulation, dwindling space and resources, and rising costs have made Lucknow rather like any other metropolitan city.

The majority of the population still depends on agriculture for survival and does not enjoy the many benefits of the modern industrial sector. The transition of the economy from agriculture to manufacturing has been haphazard, therefore, poverty and illiteracy rule Lucknow. A decline in prosperity began almost hundred years ago as food-crop production dropped and the once-booming handicraft and handloom activities shrank. By the dawn of the twenty-first century, Lucknow had lost much of its sparkle. Once a precious jewel in the British crown, the region has been gradually reduced to one of the poorest places in the world.

Perhaps it is easier to destroy the economy, but the age-old cultural genius of the region is more resilient and far more difficult to abuse. Graciousness has not abandoned Lucknow entirely. It continues to float around the city in bits and pieces, and condescends to reveal itself on rare occasions. In whatever watered-down way, elegance and hospitality live on and surface during a moment such as this one when guests descended on the home of a host who had fallen on bad times. As the guests were welcomed at the front door, one of the youngsters of the host's family disappeared from the back entrance to the home of a neighbour to borrow milk and sugar. Within minutes, a tray arrived with a hot pot of tea accompanied by different varieties of biscuits.

Historian Saleem Kidwai points out that Abdul Halim Sharar's *Guzishta Lakhnau* (Bygone Lucknow) has been mistakenly translated as *The Last Phase of Oriental Culture*. According to Kidwai, the cultural phase that evolved in the eighteenth and nineteenth centuries in Lucknow by no means ended with the deposition of the monarch in 1856 but lingers on well into the present.

Of course, the people who travelled from house to house to sharpen kite strings and kitchen knives have disappeared. The institution of the courtesans has been reduced to common prostitution. Butchers, bakers, and vegetablewalas no longer pass by homes on a bicycle. The voices of vendors selling bangles and those wanting to card wool on a contraption as intriguing as a musical instrument have also been silenced. There was a time when professionals made regular visits to houses to rid

a shadow of the past

the feet of a corn, to cut toenails, to clean the ears of wax, and to give a head massage. These services have been replaced by manicure and pedicure treatments provided by trained beauticians. Anyone in the city can visit any shop now to buy what is needed. It is freedom, especially for women, to be able to walk the streets and around the marketplace instead of having to negotiate life from behind curtains, and half-open doors.

Life changed abruptly after the takeover of Lucknow by the British East India Company in 1856. The shock of watching the regal way of life disappear overnight created uncertainty amongst citizens who fell victim to a desperate longing for the past. Life, in the present, became unbearable for ordinary people. Since it was not possible to return to the past either, a collective sadness descended upon the city. Regret over what is not, gripped the city like a disease and sunk the Lakhnauwala into deep melancholia.

From his exile in Kolkata, Wajid Ali Shah prayed every day imploring fate to give him a glimpse of his beloved Lucknow, one last time.

The poet Tabatabai wrote in the early twentieth century that the poet is no longer witness to the charismatic congregations of the past that seem to have been swallowed up by the earth and sky of Lucknow.

Majaz saw Lucknow as a paradise of beauty and romance, and the lap of grace even in the middle of the twentieth century.

The dastango (storyteller) continued to distract fellow citizens from the miseries of the present. He used his gift with words to create in the mind's eye a different and more beautiful world. He made his audience imagine that the world of their choice was a brave one. The storyteller felt that it was his responsibility to assure society that it was not impossible to return to the good old days. He wooed the audience with an attractive use of body language, emotional rants, appropriate silences, and rhythm before walking everyone into a world full of wonder. After all, the storyteller had picked up tricks of endless possibility from the kathaks of Vrindavan. The kathaks are loved for knowing secrets that lurk in the shadows of thick forests surrounding the birthplace of Krishna. South Asia has a long tradition of oral storytelling. In Lucknow, many age-old local tales combined with the addictive storytelling forms of Persia. The repertoire of any storyteller includes exaggerated narratives of love and loss and the daring and double-dealing of characters that help in distracting audiences from the distress faced by them in real life.

Dastangoi is the art of telling a series of never-ending stories within stories collected by traders and adventurers travelling in ancient and medieval times through the Middle East, Central Asia, and the West Asian region. And the narrator of a dastan or story is the dastango. European merchants added to tales collected on the Great Silk Road between China

a shadow of the past

and the very busy port of Venice. This genre began with *The Adventures of Amir Hamza*, an Arab story concocted around the seventh century, in praise of an uncle of Prophet Muhammad. The Persians added panache to this story. With the rapid spread of Islam, the Hamza stories travelled to South Asia between the eleventh and fourteenth centuries. In the sixteenth century, Hamza made a debut at Emperor Akbar's court. His Majesty was so entertained by the story in Farsi that Indian, Persian, Turkic, and European artists were commissioned at great cost to illustrate the dastan in 1562. The 1,400 *Hamzanama* paintings took nearly a decade and a half to complete. During a dastangoi session, the storyteller stood behind the gigantic *Hamzanama* folios and with the aid of text in Farsi, explained the tales illustrated in the paintings with great drama. Most of the folios are now lost except for sixty preserved at Vienna's Museum of Applied Art in Austria. That the art so admired by Akbar was appreciated, recognized, rescued, and restored in the heart of Europe would have warmed the heart of the Mughal emperor and assured him that he was quite right to have invested in secular faith and pluralism.

Decades after the death of Akbar, the *Hamzanama* folios were defaced and found strewn all over the place. Art collectors rescued some folios from street shops and others that were being used as curtains in slums. Nadir Shah had sacked Delhi in 1739 and returned to Iran with volumes of the *Hamzanama*. When he was asked to return the art, the Persian warrior said, 'Ask for the return of all your treasures and they are yours, but not the *Hamzanama*.' In 2009, the precious folios of the *Hamzanama* were exhibited at a museum in Vienna. And I was there to witness the rare exhibit. It was a jaw-dropping experience to gaze at art from medieval times radiating timeless joy. It was a moment to marvel at all the magic that takes place when different cultures collide and vivify each other.

The many adventures of Hamza were recited in Arabic, Farsi, and later in Urdu. These stories were told orally and were very popular. In the mid-nineteenth century, some people in Lucknow felt that the Hamza stories no longer entertained and that they were silly, childish, and boring. That is how many local stories with far more colourful descriptions of local evil spirits, magicians, and sorceresses were added to the Hamza stories.

Mir Ahmed Ali was a cheeky storyteller of the time. He did not do away with Hamza entirely but transported the adventures of the Arab warrior to a brand-new landscape dotted with fresh faces and amazing talents. He called his story *Tilism-e-Hoshruba*, the land of enchantment that was peppered with instances of such glamour and dishonesty that the audience could not have enough of the shenanigans, even those that dripped with deceit.

a shadow of the past

Wrote Mir Ahmed Ali:

> The cupbearers of nocturnal revelries, the bibbers from the cup of inspiration, pour the vermilion wine of inscription into the paper's goblet.

The trickery found in the tales of Mir Ahmed Ali made him so famous that he was offered an enormous amount of money to perform at the court in Rampur. More colourful than the characters populating his stories, Mir Ahmed Ali never thought twice about using chicanery to win the heart of the audience. His entourage left for Rampur in carriages driven by oxen. With tears running down their faces, a large crowd followed the departing caravan of the storyteller till the outskirts of the city. The loudest cry over leaving Lucknow was that of Mir Ahmed Ali himself. But before he left, he chose the youthful Muhammad Amir Khan to continue to entertain audiences in Lucknow with the immensely popular Hoshruba stories. Some say that Amir Khan did a better job of dramatizing humbuggery than his master.

In the 1880s, Hoshruba enthralled Munshi Newal Kishore, owner of the first printing press in Lucknow. Kishore hired the poets Muhammad Husain Jah and Ahmed Hussain Qamar to write down, in Urdu and Farsi, the stories that they recited. Jah's father was a magician and master of several physical and occult sciences. He taught his son the different branches of science and how to use them in different combinations to awaken the spirits of the cosmic force. That is how

Jah was able to create a fantastical world of sorcery. His storytelling was out of this world probably because witchcraft had cast such a spell on his writing. That is why only Jah was able to convince his audience that it was possible for a land of smoke to thrive between heaven and earth with a sorceress and her king as its rulers.

In the real world, the nawab had been exiled and India was declared the property of Queen Victoria of England at the close of the nineteenth century. The British rulers of Lucknow saw no magic in a dastan. They had no time for storytellers and their endless, often unrelated, narratives. They rubbished the performances about wicked women and demons with multiple heads as foolish and a waste of time. They dismissed the text as neither literature nor entertainment. To them, poetry was what William Wordsworth wrote, and literature was the English novel that had a beginning, middle, and end. It was Victorian realism alone that was worthy of study and not unbelievable babble about fairies and imaginary lands. They dismissed the whimsical stories in the many volumes of the Hamza and the Hoshruba texts which were considered a treasure house of Urdu vocabulary and cultural subtleties! That is how the sun gradually set on the unique performances of the local storyteller. Audiences were also distracted by the appearance of the bioscope and similar inventions that had glamorized entertainment at the start of the twentieth century. Dastango Sheikh Tassaduq Hussain dragged the art form into the new century, before breathing his last in 1918. Hussain was followed by Mir Baqar Ali who performed till his death in 1928, after which there was silence. Not a sound more was heard from the loquacious lips of another storyteller till the 2000s, when historian Mahmood Farooqui discovered forty-six volumes of *Dastan-e-Amir Hamza* in the library of the late Shamsur Rahman Faruqi, his poet-uncle and Urdu critic. The scholar discovered that the storyteller would first spend time amongst ordinary people. Once he had collected a bagful of information from the public, his job was to return to court and, from memory, inform the ruler what his subjects were saying about him. Later, the storyteller enriched his repertoire by including many marvellous stories of adventure, romance, and magic that amused the king and his majesty's courtiers. These delightful stories were heard for sheer pleasure and served no religious purpose.

The storyteller has risen from the ashes to the joy of the audience. Once again, the city echoes with 'suno, suno, suno' and other calls by the dastango that warn citizens about those who might be taking the city for yet another ride…'Hoshiyaar, khabardaar'. (Beware)…

SEVEN

Making up Stories

It is now time for the Dastan-e-Lucknow to end but not without mention of Himanshu Bajpai. To know more about Himanshu Bajpai, we must return to Shamsur Rahman Faruqi, the scholar who introduced the magic of dastangoi or storytelling to Mahmood Farooqui. Listening to his uncle talk about the sixteenth-century art of Urdu storytelling had floored Farooqui and he decided to make it a full-time profession.

Since 2005, Mahmood Farooqui has introduced dastangoi to many enthusiasts and Himanshu Bajpai is one of them. Himanshu took lessons from Farooqui and now stages spectacular performances like *Dastan-e-Lucknow* and *Dastan-e-Awaargi*. The second story is inspired by the life and works of Majaz, the most romantic and revolutionary poet of the twentieth century.

But who is Himanshu Bajpai? Perhaps he is a descendant of the community of Bajpai Brahmins in Lucknow who were close allies of Emperor Akbar? Or perhaps not. Whatever the truth, Bajpai doesn't care what caste or religion a human being belongs to. About

a shadow of the past

himself, Himanshu says that he was born a Brahmin, but that there is nothing Brahminical about him. He does not say more. He just smiles.

The close relationship of the Bajpai Brahmins to Lucknow goes back to the sixteenth century when Sheikh Abdur Rahim was appointed the first governor of Lucknow by Emperor Akbar. The Sheikh had a Brahmin wife, and he was happy to invite her relatives from the Bajpai community in Kanyakubj (Kannauj) to live in Lucknow. Here, the Brahmins were offered trusted jobs and lived in prosperity. Similar gestures of generosity, practised over centuries by community leaders are emulated and help to strengthen relationships amongst citizens. To this day, people in Lucknow seem comparatively more respectful towards each other than in many other places. This attitude is poetically called Ganga-Jamuni, similar to the confluence of the rivers Ganga and Jamuna (Yamuna) at Prayagraj, some 200 kilometres southeast of Lucknow. However, any mention of Ganga-Jamuni is met with a scoff, and dismissed as a cliché. Once upon a time, it was a well-thought-out strategy by administrators to deal with political, historical, and socio-economic differences amongst citizens of the day. In times of encounters between civilizations, the warrior's response is always to break into violence and war. On the other hand, the intelligentsia looks for more creative ways to adapt. The rulers of Lucknow in the nineteenth century were an attractive blend of warriors and wise men.

The greatest achievement of the rulers of Lucknow was to encourage harmony amongst the diverse population of the city that was home to different communities. The rulers were respectful of the aspirations of both Muslim and Rajput landlords, as well as the non-Rajput Hindu elites. That way, the city enjoyed considerable peace although it was another story on the battlefield.

One day, over a cup of coffee, Bajpai told me that he was born in a locality where some of his neighbours did not practice the same religion as his family. But his bond with them remains strong because they share the same interests in life and speak the same language. Growing up in Lucknow's Raja Bazaar meant celebrating all the festivals amongst Hindus, Muslims, and Christians. Bajpai refuses to see himself only as a Hindu. He feels more like a tiny, but important, piece of a larger puzzle. He is a healthy Raja Bazaari, one of the most colourful residential-cum-commercial parts of the old city. Here Shiva devotees may at one time have refused to share salt with Naag worshippers, but had agreed with Vishnu bhakts that the begging bowl of the bhikshu looks suspicious.

Raja Bazaar was founded in the eighteenth century by Raja Tikait Rai, the Hindu Kayastha prime minister of a Shia Muslim ruler, near a road named after Victoria, Queen of England. Raja Tikait Rai made a lot of money but he also gave back to the people by providing many public services. The residence of the Kayastha prime

a shadow of the past

minister in the same neighbourhood was an open house. It does not exist anymore, but temples, water tanks, marketplaces such as Nakkhas, and a big mosque built by him still stand and are in use by ordinary citizens.

In his neighbourhood, Bajpai was particularly close to a childhood friend called Ashish whose family owned a shop in one of the by-lanes of the busy marketplace. The poet Krishn Bihari Noor came regularly to the same shop to buy cigarettes. At that time, Bajpai had no clue what a great poet Noor was. He did not know that throughout the 1950s, Noor was a lyricist in great demand in Mumbai. When he was a bit older and thought he had fallen in love, Bajpai took solace in verse. He was not even sure whether he was in love with a woman or with life. At that time, the head of the teenager was full of romance, and he had filled an entire notebook with sentimental songs of love. One day, he took his verses to Noor, who is considered the lord of lyrical ghazals. This was in 2002. Noor opened the door of his home to Bajpai, and patiently listened to him while he recited his poetry. Bajpai became a regular at Noor's house and they spent time talking for hours. It is unclear whether Noor was able to improve the quality of Bajpai's verses but the young poet learnt a lot about love and life from the talented Noor. The conversations with Noor continue to haunt and guide him. Noor had worshipped humanity. In one of his verses, he claimed that it is only perspectives that change—the light in the Kaaba is the same as the glow in Somnath.

Noor encouraged Bajpai to read regularly even as he wrote poetry. Bajpai asked the great poet what he should read and Noor replied: the story of Karbala. Noor said that this was important because the incident of Karbala that took place in 680 CE persuades human beings to remain human. To know the story of Karbala is to want to be brave and generous.

Noor passed away in 2003. Himanshu Bajpai would have liked to have spent more time with the poet. He joined the Shia College in the same neighbourhood for a graduate course in science. The college had opened, in 1923, with contributions made by the Shia Muslim elite to educate young people. He wanted to study science to please his father. But he did not fare too well in his studies. However, the three years he spent on the college campus sucked him into a cultural ambience that continues to excite him. As a child, Bajpai had participated in the annual Muharram rituals, led by Shia Muslim families and joined by the entire neighbourhood. He looked forward to Muharram, the first month of the Islamic calendar, as much as he waited for the Ramlila performances. But it is only on the campus of the Shia College that he understood the spirit of Karbala. He began to gradually identify with the political and social context of the martyrdom of Hussain at the Battle of Karbala in the seventh century. He improved his spoken Urdu. He found out more about Urdu literature on the campus that had opened in 1923 with contributions made by the Shia Muslim elite to educate young people hungry for knowledge. After his graduation, Bajpai left Lucknow for further studies in Bhopal but he did not forget Karbala. He wanted to live only in Lucknow. After finishing his studies in mass communication, he returned to Lucknow in 2009 as a writer for the *Tehelka* news magazine.

Bajpai published a book titled *Qissa Qissa Lucknowa,* in 2019, exploring ideas of syncretism in his writing. Today, he is a full-time storyteller. Every story that he prepares to perform on stage makes his fragile heart open up a little more. His desire is to enter into dialogue with as many human beings as possible beyond caste, community, and religious considerations. Bajpai has concluded that he would like nothing better than to keep alive the very precious, composite culture of Lucknow.

Back in the middle of the nineteenth century, Munshi Newal Kishore left Lahore to make a home in Lucknow. In 1858, he founded a printing press that was the first of its kind in North India. Soon Munshi's business expanded greatly. He is remembered as the guardian angel of Urdu, a Hindu in love with the Muslim way of life. Munshi immortalized much of the oral traditions of his time by making them available in print. After Lucknow's Muslim monarchy ended and the city was annexed by the British, Arab, and Farsi scholars lost their patronage. There was also a shortage of textbooks. For a long time, it was the books donated by Munshi that helped teachers and students of Islamic studies to continue with their work. Munshi published the Quran and sold it for one rupee and eight annas in 1868, making the holy book available to ordinary readers. Stories are told of Munshi providing facilities to office workers to perform vuzu, or ablutions, before starting their work on binding the holy book.

Lav Bhargava, a descendant who lives in the house built by Munshi in 1870 in the heart of Hazratganj, feels that he has inherited a lifelong appreciation for the cultures and languages of others from his ancestor. Lav is attracted to politics precisely because it gives him a platform to share his views on the benefits of communal harmony. The press built by Munshi to flag off a cultural renaissance in the country is now defunct. However, the interest that the books published by him revived in literature and the local languages continues.

As the first Indian to open a press in Lucknow, he heralded the new era of mass-produced books. He not only set printing in Arabic, Persian, and Urdu on a sound commercial footing, but also established himself as the city's first publisher of Hindi and Sanskrit books.

Mirza Asadullah Ghalib, poet laureate of the Mughal court between 1854 and 1857, however, did not think much of Lucknow or the city's poets. But Ghalib, strangely, liked Munshi and compared his good looks to the beauty of Venus. 'He is himself the conjunction of two auspicious stars, Venus and Jupiter,' raved Ghalib, who wrote to a friend that when Munshi prints a man's writing, it raises him to heaven.

a shadow of the past

'The calligraphy is so good that every word shines radiant!' Ghalib gushed about the work of Munshi. Ghalib wrote for the *Avadh Akhbar,* a daily newspaper in Urdu launched by Munshi in 1859. A few years later, when Munshi finally met Ghalib, the publisher impressed the elderly poet with his agreeable manners. Urdu had replaced Farsi as the official language in 1837. *Avadh Akhbar* did much to spread the habit of reading among ordinary people. Despite tough competition, the *Avadh Akhbar* survived till 1950.

Wrote an enthusiastic reader in 1870:

> Munshi Sahib your paper is a fountainhead of eloquence and a source of enchantment. Who am I to praise it, big words from a little mouth. Judging from the multitude of news and the acceptance on the part of our contemporaries one could rightly call it the mother of newspapers...

Munshi made sure that the premises of the *Avadh Akhbar* did not remain merely an editorial office but also served as ameeting place between ordinary readers and the city's intelligentsia, including Ratan Nath Sarshar and Mirza Hadi Ruswa. Sarshar's *Fasana-e-Azad* was serialized in *Avadh Akhbar* to popular acclaim. In 1889, Munshi published Ruswa's *Umrao Jaan Ada,* making it possible, a century later, for Rekha to play the protagonist in *Umrao Jaan,* the 1981 film directed by Muzaffar Ali.

The first English translations of Western fictional

literature appeared at the turn of the nineteenth century. Munshi met Henry Fanthome and appointed him head translator at the *Avadh Akhbar*. Born in a well-known family of poets of Indo-French origin, Fanthome had already translated *Ek Rusi Zamindar ka Kissa* from the English translation of the French novel *The Story of a Russian Landlord*. Fanthome was fluent in Persian and Urdu and composed poetry in both languages. In translating Western literature, including Shakespeare's body of work and Victorian entertainment novels, popular as leisure-time reading, Munshi hoped to give a boost to Urdu fiction.

Apart from poetry, Munshi enjoyed the oral tradition of storytelling, and loved the dastangoi performances of Muhammad Husain Jah. The enterprising Munshi hired scribes to write, translate, and compile *Tilism-e-Hoshruba*, the world's first and longest magical fantasy in Urdu and printed them between 1883 and 1893. Spread over 8,000 pages, *Hoshruba* became even more popular than the Hamza stories. It was an instant bestseller. It is the same text printed by Munshi nearly 130 years ago that resurfaced in the hands of Mahmood Farooqui—one of the most important storytellers in contemporary times, who continues to pass on the art to other artistes, including women.

Apart from being one of the most talented students of Mahmood Farooqui, Himanshu Bajpai completed a doctorate degree on *Avadh Akhbar,* Northern India's first daily launched by Munshi in colonial India. He

a shadow of the past

studied the importance of *Avadh Akhbar* as a platform for representatives of Urdu literature to publicly express their views not only on literary but also on social and political affairs, to either engage in a critique of colonialism or to extol the benefits of Western civilization.

Today, Lucknow is proud of Bajpai's great accomplishments as a storyteller. He is valued for weaving stories that try to figure out why Lucknow is the way it is and where it is headed—by telling the world the way Lucknow was in the past.

Bajpai smiles when people complain that Lucknow is no longer like it once was. He smiles some more, adding that it is not possible for Lucknow to be like it was when the nawabs had ruled. At present, Lucknow is best seen as a pale shadow of its imperial past, a chaotic, contemporary city struggling to earn the title of a smart city by improving the quality of life for its citizens.

The most precious legacy inherited by Lucknow is friendship between the city's Hindu and Muslim residents. In general, love and loyalty amongst people still exists. Lucknow is proud of the fact that its citizens did not hurt each other while riots took place in other parts of the country during Partition. After the demolition of the Babri Masjid in 1992 and during the mass murders in Gujarat in 2002, no incident of revenge or violence was reported from Lucknow.

Hundreds of stories are told about the different

ways human beings in Lucknow express their love for each other; about Muslim begums who built Hindu temples and Hindu noblemen who spent a large part of their wealth in illuminating the shrine of a beloved Sufi mystic. Who can forget Muslim monarchs reciting odes in praise of Lord Krishna and Kashmiri Pandits who have penned soul-searching poetry in Urdu? One story that is part of Bajpai's repertoire is from recent times. It is about a gentleman called Kalika Srivastava who was once a regular visitor at a local bar. Srivastava attracted attention to himself because he would ask for two drinks, despite having come alone to the bar. Every day he sat by himself in the same comfortable corner sipping from one glass, and then from the second.

When an inquisitive person asked him why he did so, Srivastava said that one drink was for Iftiqar Husain and the second one was for him. Iftiqar Husain was his childhood friend. They grew up sharing a lot of joy, including a daily peg of whisky. Srivastava was devastated when Husain left for Pakistan and he found it difficult to enjoy drinking in the absence of his friend. Eventually, Srivastava found a solution to his misery that provided him some solace. Whenever he ordered a drink for himself, he made it a habit to get a second drink in memory of Husain. One day, Srivastava was seen holding only one glass in his hand. To all those who wanted to know more, Srivastava explained that he had given up drinking on the advice of his doctor. But he continued to buy a drink in the name of Husain

a shadow of the past

as he was not aware of any medical restriction imposed upon his friend.

Human relationships continue to matter in a city that does not just tolerate fellow human beings but celebrates the presence on its soil of different people practising different cultures and religions, and speaking different languages. Patriotism and love of the land in Lucknow is always interpreted as the art of getting along with other human beings, in particular, with one's neighbours.

Monarchs throughout the nineteenth century had shown by example that it is not enough for people to merely coexist; it was essential that they be consistently respectful towards each other. It was rulers and community leaders who had taken the lead in sharing love and affection with the people. Once upon a time, love was practised in Lucknow with abandon, and in such abundance that even the air and the water here were soaked in tenderness. A deep sense of bhaichara or brotherhood was already in practice in Lucknow long before the Indian Constitution established the ideas of fraternity, liberty, and equality. For centuries, fraternity has been the number one priority in Lucknow, in the absence of which it is impossible to enjoy liberty and equality.

Today, Lucknow is covered in gloom as attempts are being made to tear fraternities apart, and to turn citizens against each other. People here have no previous experience of a state that forces its citizens to hate each other. They wonder about ways to counter organized hate that is being spread by leaders with an agenda. These politicians use religion to make political gains. They want people to believe that a rift between Hindus and Muslims is in the interest of the state's population of 200 million out of which 20 per cent is Muslim. Muslim men are accused of love jihad, of seducing Hindu women and converting them to Islam. Unemployed youngsters have been rounded up to form Romeo squads to seek out Muslim men and to punish them for being in relationships with Hindu women. In the name of protecting Hindu women, Hindu pride, and cows, armed vigilantes attack Muslim men routinely, and street mobs have lynched men and raped women in different cities of Uttar Pradesh. Rabble rousers demand a travel ban on Indian Muslims, others want to deprive Muslims of their voting rights, making them feel vulnerable and insecure.

Deepak Kabir is not Muslim. He is a Hindi poet and cultural activist who was jailed in December 2019. His crime was his concern for his friends who were arrested on 19 December 2019 for participating in a peaceful protest against the Citizenship (Amendment) Act. He went to a local police station to enquire about them. At the police station he was arrested, abused, and thrashed mercilessly. He was called a Communist and revolutionary for wearing his hair long. Deepak told me that he fought the policemen who wanted to strip him naked to check if he was circumcised like Muslim

a shadow of the past

men and only pretending to be a Hindu.

Sufi, Deepak's teenaged son, was devastated at the arrest of his father, who was repeatedly denied bail. After waiting for two weeks for his father to come home, in January 2020, Sufi wrote an open letter to Yogi Adityanath, the chief minister of Uttar Pradesh. In the letter, Sufi wished the chief minister a happy new year. He went on to say that his new year had not been happy as his father had been in jail for the past fifteen days.

> I have been taught that it is our Constitutional right to protest, to criticise the government and to raise voices against an unjust law.
>
> I am 15 years old, in these 15 years I have attended more protests and processions than the number of exams most BJP leaders have passed...
>
> The founder of Lucknow's popular Kabir Festival named after Sant Kabir, the fifteenth-century Bhakti poet, Deepak Kabir was kicked, punched and slapped in jail as if he was a criminal...
>
> I have always been part of protests. I have spent days preparing for a strike, seminar, elections or a call to fill up jails...but after every protest I have also enjoyed a sense of satisfaction. I have enjoyed freedom, laughter and joy at the return of conversation and at the thought that the world is so beautiful.... But now it seems like breathing

> space has shrunk for us ordinary people. I want nothing more from life than a few good lines of poetry, a good story, hearty laughter, endless love and sometimes estrangement...instead I find myself being dragged into the fire of a never-ending struggle.

This is what the beloved city is reduced to today. Conspicuous by their absence are the wise people who had appeared in times of distress to build bridges across sections of society. Now the city is overrun by those who are building barriers between citizens. State power is used not to curb increasing crimes against Dalits and women, not to provide shelter to the homeless, livelihoods to the jobless, healthcare to the sick, and education to the illiterate, but to curb dissent. Fear and terror are instilled in citizens in the hope that dissent will end. However, Lucknow is restless.

This collective feeling of unease cannot just be due to homelessness and joblessness. Ordinary people have lived with poverty for aeons. What the city finds more difficult to live with is hate. Despite poverty, people in Lucknow have remained gracious and committed to the idea of living together. Diversity, pluralism, the celebration of the intellect have always been welcome here. However, a lot of the grace and goodness harvested from the past is being lost.

Hopefully, this too shall pass. Meanwhile, citizens are holding on to whatever little is left of the paradise

a shadow of the past

that Lucknow once was by continuing to be kind to each other. People want to remain united as they wait for a new dawn in Lucknow. The state may not encourage unity in the city today, but citizens realize that it is now up to them, especially Hindus and Muslims, to make sure that they do not let go of each other's hands held together in undying friendship for so long.

Acknowledgements

Thank you, David Davidar, for asking me to write about Lucknow for you. It is a matter of great pride to be part of the Aleph Book Company family. Without Pujitha Krishnan, my editor, this book would not be the same. Thank you, Pujitha, for your razor-sharp editing and for responding to my Lucknow manuscript with so much love. I would like to thank the designer Bena Sareen and the illustrator, Rashmi Tyagi, for making the book look so attractive.

I am grateful to my family, and to all my friends who did not hear from me for days on end as I concentrated on writing this book for supporting me in my endeavor to recapture the essence of a city so dear to my heart.

Once again, I would like to thank my parents, Farrukh Jaffar and Syed Muhammad Jaffar, for having encouraged me since childhood to always have my say in speech as well as in writing.

Notes

Chapter One: A Garden of Eden

1 **shafaq se hain dar-o-diwar**: Mir Taqi Mir, 'shafaq se hain dar-o-diwar zard sham-o-sahar', *Rekhta.org*, available here: https://www.rekhta.org/couplets/shafaq-se-hain-dar-o-diivaar-zard-shaam-o-sahar-mir-taqi-mir-couplets/.

2 **gulshan-e-firdaus**: Nazm Tabatabai, 'mujhko samjho yaadgar-e-raftagan-e-lucknow', *Rekhta.org*, available here: https://www.rekhta.org/ghazals/mujh-ko-samjho-yaadgaar-e-raftagaan-e-lucknow-nazm-tabaa-tabaaii-ghazals/.

12 **a temple of those cults of wit, gaiety, and licentiousness**: John Pemble, *The Raj, The Indian Mutiny and the Kingdom of Oudh, 1801-1859*, available here: https://archive.org/stream/in.ernet.dli.2015.100042/2015.100042.The-Raj-The-Indian-Mutiny-And-The-Kingdom-Of-Oudh-1801-1859_djvu.txt/.

16 **All Lucknow was steeped in the pursuit of luxury**: Veena Talwar Oldenburg, *Shaam-e-Awadh: Writings on Lucknow*, New Delhi: Penguin, 2007, p. 53.

19 **buton ki gali meiin shab o roz Asaf**: Nasima Aziz, *Wandering in the Lanes of History 1700s & 1800s*, New Delhi: Supernova Publishers, 2019.

22 **So lively, lovely and vibrant is the earth, home of youth and verse, land of letters**: Translation by the author.

17 **to the world as an enigma**: Asrarul Haq Majaz, 'Khub pahchan lo asrar hun main', *Rekhta.org*, available here: https://www.rekhta.org/couplets/khuub-pahchaan-lo-asraar-huun-main-asrarul-haq-majaz-couplets/.

25 **According to the National Crime Records Bureau (NCRB) report**: Indo-Asian News Service, 'NCRB data shows soaring crime rate in UP, but cops site population as excuse', *The New Indian Express*, 12 January 2020.

28 **envy and for revenge**: Llewellyn-Jones, *A Fatal Friendship*, p. 194.

33 **The beauty of Princess Bahar**: Musharraf Farooqui, *Hoshruba: The Land and the Tilism*, Random House India, 2009.

37 **Effeminacy, cupidity and treachery:** John Pemble, *The Raj, The Indian Mutiny and the Kingdom of Oudh 1801-1859*, Random House India, 2009.

Chapter Two: Paradise of Poets

40 **Revolution will come:** Ali Sardar Jafri, 'inqalab aaega raftar se mayus na ho', *Rekhta.org*, available here: https://www.rekhta.org/couplets/inqalaab-aaegaa-raftaar-se-maayuus-na-ho-ali-sardar-jafri-couplets/.

41 **crush the world of sorrow:** Moin Ahsan Jazbi, 'ghamon ki duniya ko raund dalen nashat-e-dil paemal kar len', *Rekhta.org*, available here: https://www.rekhta.org/ghazals/gamon-kii-duniyaa-ko-raund-daalen-nashat-e-dil-paaemaal-kar-len-moin-ahsan-jazbi-ghazals/.

41 **Paradise of love:** Asrarul Haq Majaz, 'Lucknow', *Rekhta.org*, available here: https://www.rekhta.org/nazms/lucknow-asrar-ul-haq-majaz-nazms/.

42 **learnt the first principles of socialism:** Raza Naem, 'Dreamer Meets Revolutionary', *The Friday Times*, 28 August 2015, https://www.thefridaytimes.com/dreamer-meets-revolutionary/.

42 **leaders and freedom fighters:** Venkat Dhulipala, *Creating a New Medina*, New Delhi: Cambridge University Press, 2015.

43 **Don't wait for the revolution:** Asrarul Haq Majaz, 'nau-jawan se', *Rekhta.org*, available here: https://www.rekhta.org/nazms/nau-javaan-se-asrar-ul-haq-majaz-nazms/.

45 **my purpose is change:** Josh Malihabadi, 'kaam hai mera taghayyur nam hai mera shabab', *Rekhta.org*, available here: https://www.rekhta.org/couplets/kaam-hai-meraa-tagayyur-naam-hai-meraa-shabaab-josh-malihabadi-couplets/.

48 **This Progressive Movement was a spectrum of different shades of political:** Ali Sardar Jafri, 'Progressive Movement and Urdu Poetry', *South Asian Peoples Forum*, available here: http://pwa.sapfonline.org/page5.html/.

49 **touched by these hands:** Ali Sardar Jafri, 'hathon ka tarana', *Rekhta.org*, available here: https://www.rekhta.org/nazms/haathon-kaa-taraana-ali-sardar-jafri-nazms/.

49 **blood calls:** Ali Sardar Jafri, 'lahu pukarta hai', *Rekhta.org*, available here: https://www.rekhta.org/nazms/lahuu-pukaartaa-hai-ali-sardar-jafri-nazms/.

50 **my home, each particle of dust:** Ali Sardar Jafri, *PoemHunter.com*, available here: https://www.poemhunter.com/ali-sardar-jafri/biography/.

a shadow of the past

53 **Speak up, oh earth**: Asrarul Haq Majaz, 'bol! ari o dharti bol!', *Rekhta.org*, available here: https://www.rekhta.org/nazms/bol-arii-o-dhartii-bol-asrar-ul-haq-majaz-nazms/.
54 **At the age of thirty-nine**: Damani Kulkarni, 'An Urdu poet, her activist niece, and two faces of rebellion at Lucknow's Farangi Mahal', *Scroll.in*, 18 September 2017.
76 **impossible to experience joy without knowing pain**: Brij Narayan Chakbast, 'dard-e-dil pas-e-wafa jazba-e-iman hona', *Rekhta.org*, available here: https://rekhta.org/ghazals/dard-e-dil-paas-e-vafaa-jazba-e-iimaan-honaa-chakbast-brij-narayan-ghazals-1/.

Chapter Three: Beyond Borders

79 **'We enjoyed such a wide cultural experience'**: Maxine Reding nee Cline in conversation with the author in 2018.

Chapter Four: The Honey-Tongued

74 **'veiled like a dream comes the enlightened one'**: *Rekhta.org*, available here: https://www.rekhta.org/poets/arzoo-lakhnavi/all/.
75 **'Hasrat, you are fortunate in your love for the one'**: Hasrat Mohani, 'Krishn', *Rekhta.org*, available here: https://www.rekhta.org/nazms/krishn-mathuraa-ki-nagar-hai-aashiqii-kaa-hasrat-mohani-nazms/.
76 **sounds may die but that which strikes the eye**: *Rekhta.org*, available here: https://www.rekhta.org/poets/chakbast-brij-narayan/all/.
82 **Khushwant Singh once said that the tragedy of the Anglo-Indians**: Khushwant Singh, 'Book review: I. Allan Sealy's "The Trotter-Nama"', *India Today*, 15 September 1988.
84 **In a 1796 letter to a European friend, Martin wrote**: Rosie Llewellyn-Jones, *A Very Ingenious Man: Claude Martin in Early Colonial India*, Oxford University Press, 1993.

Chapter Five: Mad About Movies

93 **here amongst thorns, the Prophet's flowers**: David Mathews, *The Battle of Karbala: A Marsiya of Anis*, New Delhi:, Rupa Publications, 1994.
95 **He (Polier) found**: Aziz, *Wandering in the Lanes of History 1700s and 1800s*, p. 81.

Chapter Six: The World is My Oyster

98 **well into the present:** Aziz, *Wandering in the Lanes of History 1700s and 1800s*, p. xiii

99 **imploring fate to give him a glimpse:** Wajid Ali Shah Akhtar, 'yahi tashwish shab-o-roz hai bangale mein', *Rekhta.org*, available here: https://rekhta.org/couplets/8b77cafd-e9fd-4ea3-857f-59ad58920ece-wajid-ali-shah-akhtar-couplets/.

99 **the poet is no longer witness:** Nazm Tabatabai, 'mujhko samjho yaadgar-e-raftagan-e-lucknow', *Rekhta.org*, available here: https://rekhta.org/ghazals/mujh-ko-samjho-yaadgaar-e-raftagaan-e-lucknow-nazm-tabaa-tabaaii-ghazals/.

99 **Majaz saw Lucknow:** Asrarul Haq Majaz, 'Lucknow', *Rekhta.org*, available here: https://rekhta.org/nazms/lucknow-asrar-ul-haq-majaz-nazms/.

102 **'Ask for the return of all your treasures and they are yours':** 'Come with me to the land of enchantment!', *Lucknow Observer*, 5 July 2014.

103 **The cupbearers of nocturnal revelries:** Musharraf Farooqi, *Hoshruba: The Land and the Tilism*, Random House India, 2009.

Chapter Seven: Making up Stories

109 **the light in the Kaaba:** Krishn Bihari Noor, 'dikhai de na kabhi ye to mumkinat mein hai', *Rekhta.org*, available here: https://www.rekhta.org/ghazals/dikhaaii-de-na-kabhii-ye-to-mumkinaat-men-hai-krishn-bihari-noor-ghazals/.

112 **He is himself the conjunction of two auspicious stars:** Ulrike Stark, *An Empire of Books: The Naval Kishore Press and the Diffusion of the Printed in Colonial India*, New Delhi: Orient Blackswan Private Limited, 2009, p. 127.

113 **'The calligraphy is so good':** Ibid., p. 212.

113 **Munshi sahib your paper:** Ibid., p. 360.

114 **give a boost to Urdu fiction:** Ulrike Stark, *An Empire of Books*, p. 340.

118 **He is a Hindi poet and cultural activist who was jailed in December of 2019:** Mohita Tewari, 'UP: Poet and activist Deepak Kabir out of jail, speaks of torture by cops', *Times of India*, 10 January 2020.

118 **His crime was his concern for his friends who were arrested on 19 December 2019:** Mohita Tewari, 'UP: Poet and activist Deepak Kabir out of jail, speaks of torture by cops', *Times of India*, 10 January 2020.

118 **He was called a Communist and a revolutionary for keeping his hair long:** Mohita Tewari, 'UP: Poet and activist Deepak Kabir out of jail, speaks of torture by cops', *Times of India*, 10 January 2020'

119 **I have been taught that it is our Constitutional right:** Puja Awasthi, 'You've put fear inside children. Congratulations on every undemocratic thing you have done', *The Week*, 4 January 2020.